A Layman's Commentary

Volume 8

General Epistles

Hebrews, James, 1 and 2 Peter,
1, 2 and 3 John, Jude,
Revelation

John Devine

BALBOA.
PRESS
A DIVISION OF HAY HOUSE

Balboa Press books may be ordered through booksellers or by contacting:

Balboa Press
A Division of Hay House
1663 Liberty Drive
Bloomington, IN 47403
www.balboapress.com.au
1-(877) 407-4847

ISBN: 978-1-4525-2437-5 (sc)
ISBN: 978-1-4525-2438-2 (e)

Printed in the United States of America

Balboa Press rev. date: 06/30/2014

CONTENTS

General Epistles

These nine general letters were written to the early churches by leaders and apostles who were eye witnesses or associates and spoke from their own experience of Jesus. While there may have been specific locations in mind they are of general application to all believers and include words of instruction and encouragement for victorious living. They conform with the Gospels and the letters of Paul.

Hebrews explains the connection of the Old Testament with the First Coming of Jesus. Revelation describes the fulfillment of all things with the Second Coming of Jesus.

The Epistles were not written as doctrine or systematic theology but as letters to groups of believers to address issues. However they provide a significant contribution to the doctrine of the early Christian Church.

Hebrews

Introduction – In the years after the resurrection and ascension many Jewish people recognized Jesus as the Messiah, Savior and Lord. The letter to the Hebrews is an important doctrinal statement written to encourage them to hold their faith under persecution. It also presented the facts of the Gospel of the good news about Jesus to help Jews understand the superiority of the New Covenant. The name `Hebrews' identifies the intention of the author to go beyond the Mosaic Covenant back to Abraham and the roots of faith in the one true God (Eber was the first of the Hebrews Gen 11:16).

Intense persecution developed in Israel as Jews revolted against Roman rule culminating in AD 70 in the destruction of Jerusalem and the Temple by the Romans bringing an end to the Levitical Sacrificial System.

Author – An unidentified Jew who accepted Jesus as the Messiah as a result of the teachings of the apostles - eyewitnesses of Jesus *who actually heard the Lord speak 2:3.* A respected leader in the early church, well educated in the Old Testament and Jewish faith and a well known associate of Timothy 13:23. The teaching is consistent with other New Testament authors.

Period – Written to Jewish Christians around AD 65 (Temple sacrifices were still being made 8:4) - from Italy v24.

Theme - The Superiority of the Gospel The Gospel of the Lord Jesus Christ is the fulfilment and completion of God's plan of salvation and redemption for all peoples of the world -

• Jesus is superior to the Old Testament leaders both in his Person and work

• The New Covenant is superior in all respects to the Old Covenant making the Old obsolete. The Old Covenant was physical and a shadow of the New Covenant which is spiritual and eternal.

• Those who enter the New Covenant have a privileged position including access into the Most Holy Presence of God! They also have a responsibility to live transformed lives through the power of the Holy Spirit.

• There is no ground for further revelation regarding salvation!

Special Features – Hebrews makes a systematic comparison of the Old Covenant received through Moses with the New Covenant mediated by

Jesus Christ showing his superiority to all beings - the prophets, angels, man, Moses, Aaron and Joshua.

A detailed study considers the lives of the Patriarchs and other great people of God to show that they were each accepted as righteous before God, not by their deeds or rituals but because of their faith – they believed God and responded to that belief.

There are five admonitions to go on to maturity in faith, service and rest – based on the privelidged position we have now received through Christ.

SUMMARY
The Superior Person of Jesus Christ 1:1 to 7:28
The Superior Nature of the New Covenant 8:1 to 9:28
The Symbol of the Tabernacle 10:1-18
Our Privileged Position 10:9 to 10:39
Hallmarks of Faith 11:1 to 12:17
A Kingdom that Cannot be Shaken 12:18 to 13:25

THE SUPERIOR PERSON OF JESUS CHRIST

1:1-3 **God has spoke by His Son** The progressive revelation of God's plan of salvation and redemption for mankind delivered through the prophets has been recorded in the Old Testament. It has now reached completion with the coming of his Son Jesus. God spoke in the past through the prophets but now he has spoken by his Son Is 49:6,7.

God has also more fully revealed his Son in Person as he foretold in the prophetic Scriptures 5:4; Is 9:6; Lk 1:35. It is this intervention of God in the affairs of the finite world by sending his Son in the form of a human that distinguishes the Bible message from all other philosophies and beliefs and makes it imperative that each person make a decision regarding the Person and work of Jesus.

The Son of God is superior to the prophets and patriarchs because –
• He has been appointed heir of all things from eternity and is now exalted to the right hand of the Father Eph 1:9,10; Phil 2:9
• God made the universe through the Son - as partaker in the Godhead the Son was intimately involved with the Holy Spirit in the creation of all things Gen 1:2,26 - through him all things were made Jn 1:1-3; Col 1:16
• The Son radiates God's glory and is the exact representation of his being Col 1;15. We see the full nature and character of God the Father in the Son as he appeared on earth Jn 1:14

- As the Father is consciously involved in upholding the universe so the Son also sustains all things by his powerful Word Acts 17:28; Col 1:17. God completed the work of creation but still maintains the creation by his active involvement - otherwise it would revert to nothing from which it was created. This upholding work is undertaken with the Son Gen 2:1-3; Jn 5:17
- He provided lasting purification for sins - the sacrifice of Jesus resulted in complete and permanent removal of the offence of sin before God for the faithful believer 2Cor 5:21 - this could not be achieved under the Old Covenant
- He is the author and finisher (perfecter) of our faith 12:2
- He is now seated at the right hand of the Majesty in heaven with all authority given to him in heaven and on earth - he will judge the people of the earth Mt 28:18; Phil 2:9-11.

1:4-14 **The Deity of Jesus** He has eternal equality within the Godhead with the Father and the Holy Spirit Jn 1:1; 2Cor 13:14. This could not have been known except by revelation.

Angels are spiritual beings created before the material world as messengers of God to carry out his will Gen 28:12,13; 32:1; Job 1:6; Mt 4:11; 24:31. They are holy beings who act in defense of believers Ps 91:11,12; Mt 18:10. There are also fallen angels against whom we must contend Is 14:12-15; Eph 2:1-3; 6:12,13.

The Son of God is superior to the angels because -
- Jesus is recognized to be the Son of God by God the Father v5; Ps 2:7. The eternal deity of the Son is revealed in Scripture Jn 1:14: 1Jn 5:11-13.
- Jesus is worshiped by angels who serve those who inherit salvation v6,13,14; 1Pet 3:22
- Jesus will reign over mankind (and angels) forever in an eternal kingdom of righteousness and joy v8,9; Ps 45:6,7; Is 9:7
- The creation will be changed (rolled up like paper) and the kingdom of the Son will be eternal v10-12; Is 34:4; Rev 22:3-5
- After his redemptive work on the cross Jesus has been restored to his pre-creation exaltation at the right hand of the Father v13; Ps 110:1. This prophetic word of king David was acknowledged by Jesus Mt 22:41-46.

2:1-4 **First Admonition** The first of five exhortations is given not to neglect the revelation of the New Covenant. It was revealed by Jesus in his life, death and resurrection and verified by the many who saw and heard him after he rose again from the dead Jn 20:1-31; Acts 1:1-3. There were also many confirming miracles performed by the early believers as a result of the gifts distributed by the Holy Spirit and miracles do occur even today through the same gifts of the Holy Spirit v4.

If Israel lost their nationhood and went into exile for not keeping the Old Covenant *how shall we escape if we ignore such a great salvation? v3.* There are many who are in danger of neglecting or ignoring the message of Jesus Christ today.

2:5-18 Family of God That man was made in the image of God shows the immense importance of mankind to God –

• *You made him a little lower than the angels v7* - man was given rule over the earth v7; Gen 1:28

• *Put everything under his feet v8* – mankind has a glorious future not yet fulfilled

• *But we see Jesus v9* - to redeem mankind it was necessary for Jesus to take on human form 'being made in human likeness' to represent us and experience death for all people v9. By taking part in our humanity the Son of God rescued us and destroyed the power of death and the devil v14; Col 2:13-15

• *Now crowned with glory and honor v9* – we now, by faith, see Jesus in his glorified state with everything put under his feet Phil 2:5-11. This gives us a foretaste of the future God has prepared for us in eternity with all things under our feet v8

• *Bringing many sons to glory v10* - in order to bring us into God's family it was necessary for Jesus to become like us and to suffer on our behalf. This is the wonder of the incarnation – that the eternal Son of God should empty himself and take on human form – becoming truly God and truly man, in order that we might receive eternal life!

• *Both the one who makes men holy and those who are made holy are of the same family v11* - we are now of the same family - born again by the will and power of God Jn 1:10-13. Jesus is pleased to call us 'brothers' - this was all confirmed and now can be understood in the prophetic word! v12,13.

Born Again Just as we were born into the physical world which is finite so in order to obtain everlasting life we must be 'born again' into the spiritual realm of God which is eternal. This occurs by the operation of the Holy Spirit when we acknowledge our sins, confess and repent of them and accept Jesus as our Savior and Lord. He died on the cross so

that he might remove the offense of our sins before God and provide the means whereby we might receive eternal life v14; Jn 3:5-8; 1Jn 5:11,12.
As our high priest he brought us into God's family - he made atonement for the sins of the people - so that we will share his glory in the world to come v17; Rom 8:17. And having experienced our trials he is able to help us when we are tempted, to overcome or avoid the temptation v18; 1Cor 10:13.

Atonement means to remove the offense of sin before God so that the offender can be cleansed, forgiven and become reconciled with God – brought back into relationship.

3:1-6 **The Perfection and Finality of the New Covenant** The Old Covenant received by Moses on Mt Sinai was a shadow of things to come.

The Son of God is superior to Moses because -
• **Builder of the House** Moses the great lawgiver spoke with God 'face to face' and was held in highest honor. He delivered the people from bondage and brought them to God. While he was faithful to God yet he was only a member of God's house. Jesus has greater honor because he is the builder of the house v2-6. The faithful believer is also a member of that house 1Pet 2:4-6
• **New Birth and Freedom from the Power of Sin** Moses could not achieve new life for the people so they failed through lack of faith and continued sin. Jesus not only achieved salvation for us he overcame the power of sin and provided the indwelling Presence of the Holy Spirit so we could serve God freely. Having 'seen' Jesus we can 'fix our eyes and thoughts' on him, the apostle and high priest whom we confess v1; 2:9; Col 3:1-3. This is how we are able to live a victorious and effective life.

3:7-19 **Second Admonition** A further encouragement is given to hold on to faith and not let the heart become hardened as happened to the people both in the wilderness and in the Promised Land - they were excluded from God's 'rest' v11. Jesus said do not worry about anything - life, food, clothes Mt 6:25-32. Such rest is available and it comes through faith in Christ alone Mt 6:33. The people of Israel were not able to enter into the rest of God because of unbelief - lack of faith in God, his promises and his Word. They spent 40 years in the wilderness and most died there v17; Num 14:21-23.

4:1-11 **The Rest of God** To enter God's rest is to accept the blessings of his Presence, set free from the anxieties and striving of life v10. This rest is based on who we know God to be and comes to those who believe in Jesus as Savior committing their ways to him as Lord v1. Israel did not enter God's rest because of unbelief - their inability to trust God 3:11,19. We also have all of God's great promises but they will be of no value to us unless we combine them with faith and application v2.

While Joshua could give the people their inheritance in the Promised Land he was unable to give them living faith and belief in God and his Word. Victory comes through Jesus 2Cor 15:57.

The Son of God is superior to Joshua because -
• we who believe have the opportunity to enter that rest provided we heed his voice and do not harden our hearts - we must appropriate God's promises in our daily walk through faith v3,7; Rom 4:16
• we have assurance of salvation and eternal life 1Jn 5:11,12
• we have a personal, living relationship with God through Jesus 10:19-22 - we have freedom from the burden of sin, works and self-justification v10; Col 1:13,14
• we rest in the midst of the turmoil and anxiety of daily life Mt 11:28-30 - we have every spiritual blessing in Christ, in the heavenly realm Eph 1:3

This rest means - after having done all we reasonably can, to then be able to leave the matter with the Lord and find peace. This indeed, is the gift of God! Jn 14:27; 16:33.

4:12,13 **The Word of God is vital** to entering and remaining in the rest of God. We are born again by the Word of God 1Pet 1:23. We enter God's rest as we appropriate all the blessings and promises. We grow in our relationship with God through Christ as we feed on his Word daily which transforms our minds and lives - it is more important than our daily bread Job 23:12.

The Word is like the surgeon's scalpel - as we read it daily we are laid bare on the operating table before God and he moulds, shapes, strengthens and equips us for our daily tasks - he corrects, reproves and removes those areas that cause offence and impede our effectiveness Rom 12:2; 2Tim 3:16.

***4:14* Jesus the Son of God** Jesus declared that he is the Son of God Mt 26:63-65. This is affirmed by the New Testament writers Rom 1:4; 2Cor 1:19; 1Pet 1:2,3; 1Jn 1:3.

***4:14-16* The Great High Priest** Jesus as our high priest has gone into the Presence of God. He now calls us to enter God's Presence with confidence where he will provide all we need to live a joyful and effective life. This means we grow in our daily walk with God as we seek him with all our heart Jn 15:1-8.

***5:1-10* The Role of the High Priest** In the Old Covenant the high priest was appointed to represent the people before God. His task was to repeatedly offer sacrifices for sin for himself and the people demonstrating the awful offense of sin before God.

The Son of God is superior to Aaron because –
* the first high priest Aaron could not remove the stain of sin v3
* Jesus offered himself becoming the source of eternal salvation for all who obey him being of the superior order of Melchizedek v6-10; 7:1-3
* Jesus was made prefect through suffering v8.

In suffering Jesus showed us that the problems of life have a purpose - to develop our character and increase our obedience and trust in God. Suffering is to be expected in the fallen world. Jesus set us an example in that he suffered without wrongdoing and on our behalf 2Cor 8:9. This helps understand why people suffer. When we look back everything we learned was through affliction.

That Jesus had to suffer is a profound mystery. It was necessary for him to suffer and die to pay the penalty for our sin. *God made him who had no sin to be sin for us, so that in him we might become the righteousness of God 2Cor 5:21.* He had to experience everything that we experience to be like us 4:15. He therefore could bear the burden of our sin and console us in our need. His greatest suffering was on the cross - as he bore the sin of the world darkness covered the land and he cried out *'My God, why have you forsaken me' Mt 27:45,46* - he shrank from separation from God, a fate that awaits all who reject salvation.

***5:11-14* Third Admonition – Spiritual Growth** As we have this new relationship with God through Jesus we are encouraged to grow up - not to remain on the elementary truths of God's Word (milk) but to go on to maturity (solid food). We are to grow strong spiritually and become effective in the kingdom Col 2:6,7. We are to go beyond doctrine to application of the spiritual principles - to experience and active service.

6:1-3 The Foundations of Faith - elementary teachings about Christ involve repentance, faith, baptisms, the Spirit, gifts of the Spirit, resurrection and eternal judgment v1-3. We should move on from these teachings to the deeper things of effective service through study of the Word and fellowship in the Holy Spirit.

6:4-8 Moving on to Maturity There is much to learn as we grow in our relationship with God through Jesus. But it is hard to explain these things if we are slow to learn, still struggling with the basic principles and not applying them in our daily walk. Instead we need to become mature and should be teaching others. The new birth is not the end but the beginning.

Discipleship Jesus told the disciples to make disciples - teaching them to obey everything he had commanded them Mt 28:18-20. This means a life committed to the service of the kingdom of God. Our attitude should be to seek to lead everyone we meet to Christ. If they are already born again our aim should be to strengthen them in their walk with him Col 1:28. We each have a gift of the Holy Spirit for this purpose, especially the gift of encouragement Rom 12:6,8.

We must not be careless in the things of God but treat our privileged position with respect and diligence. Those who turn or fall away after experiencing the things of God will have difficulty in returning because they are crucifying Christ again by their actions and in their hearts v4.

6:9-12 We Inherit God's Promises - through work and love, faith and patience we contribute to God's people.

6:13-20 God's Promises are Sure God gave his word to Abraham who accepted what was promised - that he would have many descendants, although he could not see it. He accepted God's Word. Now we see that blessing spreading through all nations of the world. We can have absolute confidence in the things God has promised to us through his Son Jesus who has become a high priest forever after the order of Melchizedek v20.

7:1-10 The Eternal High Priest Melchizedek suddenly appeared to Abraham Gen 14:18. He was king of Jerusalem and priest of God indicating that God was at work in people outside the Bible account. Abraham recognized and honored Melchizedek giving him a tenth of everything. Melchizedek had no pre-history and no further activity in the Bible – little is known about him. He was a special priest of God

Most High without known human appointment. His name means king of righteousness and king of peace (Salem) 7:1-3. For these reasons he prefigures Jesus who has no beginning and end, is the great High Priest and also the Prince of Peace.

7:10-14 Human Perfection could not be achieved through the Levitical priesthood v11 – the law made nothing perfect v19. The high priest had to offer sacrifices daily until he was replaced through death. Jesus was descended from Judah, the line of king. He also received the anointing of priesthood v14.

7:15-28 The High Priest who meets our need Because he is holy, blameless, pure, set apart from sinners and exalted above the heavens he could sacrifice for the sins of all people once for all when he offered himself v26,27. He rose again from death demonstrating an indestructible life v16 proving that he is a priest in the order of Melchizedek forever. David foretold this of the Messiah Ps 110:4. Jesus as high priest now intercedes for us before God and so is able to save forever those who come to God through him v25. Jesus our high priest is perfect - forever v27.

THE SUPERIOR NATURE OF THE NEW COVENANT

8:1-13 The New Covenant The Tabernacle where the high priest served was handed down to Moses in the Old Covenant and represented the Presence of God among the people Ex 25:8; 40:34-38. This was a copy of the real spiritual sanctuary in heaven v2 – *all things in the Old Covenant served as a copy and a shadow of what is in heaven v5*. Temple sacrifices were still being made at the time of writing v4.

The ministry of the Son of God is superior to the ministry of the high priest because -
• the ministry of Jesus and the New Covenant are based on greater promises v8-12; Mt 3:16,17; 17:5.
God foretold that a New Covenant was required Jer 31:31-34 -
• it would be different to the old one that had been broken v9
• it would require an inner change in the minds and hearts of the people v10
• it would be for all believing people 12:23; Rev 5:9,10.
The Old Covenant was obsolete and would soon disappear v13.
In the New Covenant God gives the believer new life – with the Law of God in their minds and written on their hearts v10. This occurs through

the new birth and the filling of the Holy Spirit when we place our faith in Jesus.

9:1-10 The Old Covenant The regulations for worship required the high priest to enter the Most Holy Place once only each year with the blood of an animal shed for his own sin and for the sins of the people. This sacrifice was not able to cleanse the conscience of the people v7,9. The way for the people to come into God's Presence was not yet available while the first Tabernacle was standing v8. The Temple, built by Solomon and rebuilt by Herod replaced the Tabernacle built by Moses. These outward displays were about to be replaced by a new order v10.

9:11-28 The Perfect Sacrifice Jesus Christ as high priest entered the Most Holy Place, the heavenly sanctuary, once for all by his own blood obtaining eternal redemption for those who believe in him. The good things are already here! v11,12.

The New Covenant mediated by the Son of God is superior to the Old Covenant mediated through Moses because -
• it has secured the promised eternal inheritance by the blood of Jesus showing the supreme worth of his offering v12
• it has cleansed us so we may serve the living God v14.

Jesus as eternal high priest is now in the real Presence of God v24-26. He was sacrificed once to take away the sins of many and will appear again to bring salvation to those who are waiting for him v28. He is *the Lamb of God who takes away the sin of the world Jn 1:29;* 1Cor 5:7; Rev 5:6.

Jesus confirmed the New Covenant at the Lord's Supper as he celebrated the Passover on the night before he was crucified – he took the common bread and table wine as Moses had done when he introduced the Passover Covenant -

• **This is my body** - at the first Passover a lamb was sacrificed signifying the giving of a life to redeem the people from bondage - a life for a life Ex 12:6; 21:23. Jesus said *'This is my body given for you' Lk 22:19*

• **This is my blood** - at the first Passover blood of the sacrificed lamb was placed on the doorpost to avert the wrath of God - it is the blood that makes atonement for one's life Ex 12:7; Lev 17:11. Jesus said *'This cup is the New Covenant in my blood which is poured out for you' Lk 22:20*

• We have been redeemed *with the precious blood of Christ, a Lamb without blemish 1Pet 1:19,20.*

The first Passover Covenant was held annually to commemorate the deliverance of the people from bondage in Egypt. So we celebrate the New Covenant to remember that Jesus died and rose again to deliver us from sin and death as often as we choose *to proclaim the Lord's death until he comes 1Cor 11:23-26*.

Because of the completeness of the New Covenant there is nothing more that could be added - the full, perfect, sufficient, sacrifice has made salvation and the means of attaining eternal life final and assured! v28.

THE SYMBOL OF THE TABERNACLE

10:1-18 The New Replaced the Old The Mosaic Covenant could not cleanse the people and had to be offered repeatedly - daily and annually. Jesus, by one sacrifice has made perfect forever those who are being made holy v14. Their sins are forgiven and there is no longer any sacrifice for sin v18. God's mercy wiped out, obliterated the debt of sin Acts 3:19; Col 2:13-14. They become members of a new kingdom not just for Israel but for people of all nations. With the coming of the New the Old was wrapped up in a few years with the destruction of the Temple by the Roman general Titus in AD 70 and the whole of Jerusalem by Roman Emperor Hadrian in AD 135. This confirmed that the Temple and the old order were no longer required 8:13.

WHAT WAS THE TABERNACLE? How did it apply?

God always seeks relationship with mankind - with Adam, Enoch, Noah Gen 3:8,24; 5:22-24; 6:8,9. God chose Abraham, Isaac and Jacob Ex 3:6. God chose to dwell with the people as they were delivered from Egypt – *Have them make a sanctuary for me, and I will dwell among them Ex 25:8;* 40:34-38.

This was an illustration for the present time. It was a shadow of the relationship which we now have 9:8-10.

There were eight stages – Ex 25:1 to 27:21

1. The Courtyard Ex 27:9 – 45 m x 23 m x 2 m high - there was only one entry to the Presence of God – representing conviction and repentance of sin – the initial approach to God. Jesus said 'I Am the Door' Jn 10:7

2. The Altar Ex 27:1 - required for the sacrifice for forgiveness of sin – representing the new birth. Jesus said 'I Am the Good Shepherd – I lay down my life for the sheep' Jn 10:11

3. The Laver Ex 30:17 - required for cleansing – representing sanctification. Jesus said 'I Am the Vine - you are made clean by the Word' Jn 15:1-3

4. The Tabernacle Ex 26:1-37 – 14 m x 4.5 m x 5 m - sealed from external light. Only the priests could go in. We need to go on with the Lord!

5. The Lamp Ex 25:31 - outside was the light and influence of the world – inside the influence of the world was excluded – inside there was only one light, representing the Presence and filling of the Holy Spirit. Jesus said 'I Am the Light of the world – you will never walk in darkness' Jn 8:12

6. The Show Bread Ex 25:23-30 - manna – representing all our daily provision. Jesus said 'I Am the Bread of life' Jn 6:35

7. The Altar of Incense Ex 30:1 – representing prayer rising to the Throne – our daily walk in communion with God. Jesus said 'I Am the Way, the Truth and the Life' Jn 14:6

8. The Most Holy Place Ex 26:31-34 – 4.5 m x 4.5 m x 5 m high - with the Ten Commandments, the Ark and the Mercy Seat - representing the Presence of God. The Curtain separated man from the Presence of God. The high priest could only enter once each year on Atonement Day Ex 25:17; Lev 16:34; 17:11. Jesus opened the way for believers to enter the Presence of God now and eternally. He said 'I Am the Resurrection and the Life' Jn 11:25.

The Heavenly Tabernacle
The first Tabernacle was a representation of the real Presence of God 9:6-10. The real, spiritual, perfect Tabernacle is in heaven 9:11; Rev 13:6; 15:5; 21:3.

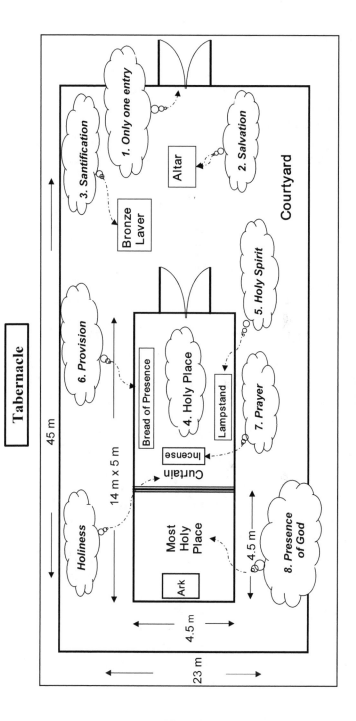

Tabernacle

Hebrews

What happened on that first Easter? Jesus celebrated the Passover on Thursday night (beginning of the Jewish Friday, at 6 pm.). Passover was determined by calendar on the 14th day of the month of Nisan - the Day of Preparation, and the meal was taken at twilight, after 6pm that night Ex 12:6. If it fell on Friday it coincided with the normal Saturday Sabbath making it a Special Sabbath Jn 19:31. Jesus held Passover on the Thursday night knowing he would be arrested before the official time. On Friday the Day of Preparation he was crucified at 9 am Jn 19:42.

When Jesus Died At 12 noon the land was in darkness for three hours as Jesus experienced complete separation from his Father Mt 27:45,46. At this time the people were taking their lambs up to the Temple to be sacrificed within one km of Calvary - as the Lamb of God was hanging on the cross. As he died at 3 pm Jesus cried out 'It is finished' Jn 19:30.

The Curtain torn At the moment Jesus died the veil in the Temple separating the Most Holy Place, entered only by the high priest once each year, was torn from top to bottom. This indicated that the way into the Presence of God was now made possible by the death of his Son and was now open to those who come to God through Jesus Mt 27:51.

OUR PRIVILEGED POSITION - our superior covenant
    10:19-21 **We have direct access to the Presence of God -**
• *Therefore* – because of all that has gone before – all that God has done for us in Christ v19
• *we have confidence to enter the Most Holy Place v19* – we can go in to the very Presence of God – all restrictions removed
• *by the blood of Jesus, by a new and living way opened for us through the curtain, that is, his body* - based on the finished work of Jesus v20
• *we have a great high priest over the house of God v21*
• *let us draw near to God v22* – approach the Presence of God.

Moses was told not to draw near to God because the offense of sin had not yet been removed Ex 3:5. Despite this God granted him a 'face to face encounter'. As a result of the sacrifice of Jesus we are now encouraged to draw near to God! We have confidence to encounter this face to face experience at any time. It will become more real and intimate as we seek the Lord with all our heart 2Cor 3:13-18. David knew this experience of seeking the face of the Lord Ps 27:4,8,14; 63:1-8; 84:1-12.

We do not have because we do not seek Jer 29:11-14.

We now view the layout of the Tabernacle in two ways –

- it is a measure of our progress and development as a believer
- it is a pattern for our prayer - our approach to God.

10:22-25 Our Privilege as Priests - Jesus has made us priests to serve God Rev 1:6.

The Old Covenant invited the people to be a kingdom of priests and a holy nation; God's chosen treasured possession Ex 19:4-6. **It was conditional** on obeying the Ten Commandments. God would show himself holy through the people to the nations Ezk 36:23. They failed through unbelief and disobedience 4:1-3.

In the New Covenant we who have faith in Jesus are *a chosen people, a royal priesthood, a holy nation, a people belonging to God that you may declare the praises of him who called you out of darkness into his wonderful light 1Pet 2:9,10*; Rev 5:9,10. **This is unconditional** – based on faith alone. As members of the royal priesthood we have the privilege of serving God by our lives - our worship, prayer, thankfulness, witness and service.

Eleven priestly guidelines are given - these are instructions which will allow us to pursue and maintain strong spiritual growth and victorious living -

Let us draw near to God v22 – we have unrestricted entrance to enter the Presence of God at any time – we need to go in!

Let us hold unswervingly to the hope we profess v23 – we can resist the devil's doubts and he will flee from us Jas 4:6,7.

Let us spur one another on towards love and good works v24 – we must motivate each other in spiritual disciplines and ministry.

Let us not give up meeting together v25 – in small groups in mutual ministry – Jesus is in the midst of two or three who meet in his name Mt 18:20.

Let us encourage one another v25 – we must mutually exercise this gift of the Holy Spirit – enthusiasm is infectious Pro 27:17.

10:26-39 Fourth Admonition With our high calling and the cost to achieve it we live a worthy life - persevering in witness in spite of hardship, resistance and persecution Phil 3:14.

HALLMARKS OF FAITH

Some see science as the rigid dogma of those who reduce everything to a materialistic world. The five senses used to investigate physical phenomenon are only half the human being – they choose to ignore experience and spiritual perception.

11:1 **The Realm of Faith** The New Covenant is based on faith in Jesus. Faith is described as substance, evidence, reality. These are the tools of natural science in the physical world. They are applied in the spiritual dimension and translate as hope and expectation into the physical realm - the eyes with which we 'see' the spiritual world - the means by which our hopes become reality v1.

Faith is 'believing God' – who he is and what he says - in his Word and through the Holy Spirit.

11:2 **Faith is evidenced by our response** We are commended before God when we act in faith v2.

11:3 **All things came from nothing** *By faith we understand that the universe was formed at God's command so that what is seen was not made out of what was visible.* Science now acknowledges (since 1920's) that the universe was created out of nothing - that there was a moment, a singularity, when there was nothing – no matter, no space, no time, no energy, no radiation, no heat. The first law of Thermodynamics identifies that total energy (a fixed amount) appeared at the beginning out of nothing from which matter then occurred (according to $E = mc^2$) together with the four energy forces that now hold the universe together Col 1:17. The source of this total energy is unknown without revelation. Faith recognizes God as the source of this total energy and that all things physical came from his command Rom 4:17. It is confirmation of God's revelation that the writer to the Hebrews could record this scientific statement around AD 65.

11:6 *Without faith it is impossible to please God* In order to have an encounter with God it is necessary to have a desire to know him. One must accept the possibility of God's existence and then make a genuine effort to search for him.

11:4-38 **Examples of Faith** To confirm the importance of faith in the life of the individual believer examples are drawn from people of the past - those who have gone before us. We learn much about God, his nature and his dealings with mankind, by studying the Old Testament 1Cor 10:11; Lk 24:44-46. We will also learn much about life and our relationship with God.

A list starts at the beginning of the Bible to identify those who were accepted by God because of their faith and not by what they did or achieved – *they believed God and it was counted to them as righteousness Rom 4:3.* It is not about them and what they did but about the common principle of faith and how it works v6. They each had a living relationship with God and acted on what God told them – *they were still living by faith when they died v13.* Faith is the foundation and the motivating principle for the believer's life. We too, like them must know God personally and respond to him in faith. Faith opens us to the power of God and frees us to achieve great things for him -

• Abel by faith offered the blood sacrifice to God v4; Gen 4:4
• Enoch believed that he would not face death v5; Gen 5:22-24
• Faith defined – believe God exists and that he rewards those who earnestly seek him v6
• Noah built the ark at God's request v7; Gen 6:9,27
• Abraham left his comfortable city home in Ur to dwelt in a foreign land in tents, in response to God's request v8; Gen 12:1
• Abraham believed the promise of God and received a son in his old age v11,12; Gen 21:1-5
• The ultimate test came when Abraham was called to offer his son – as a result of his response he became the father of the faithful v17-19; Gen 22:1,2,15-18; Rom 4:16,18
• Isaac accepted God's plan to chose Jacob v20; Gen 27:33
• Jacob chose the two sons of Joseph to receive the Covenant blessing v21; Gen 48:11-20
• Joseph despite his great service to God and his people was counted as faithful by his intention to be buried in the Promised Land v22; Gen 50:24-26
• Moses' parents acted to save their son in faith v23; Ex 2:1-4
• Moses obeyed God when called to lead the people out of Egypt. When he had tried in his own strength to accomplish the purposes of God he came to realize that he must submit all to God in faith v24-28; Ex 2:14; 5:1
• By faith Israel escaped through the Red Sea v29; Ex 14:29-31
• By an act of faith the walls of Jericho fell v30; Jos 6:20
• Rahab acted in faith choosing to follow God v31; Jos 6:25
• Gideon was called by God to go against the Midianite army with a reduced band of men to demonstrate faith in God Jud 7:2
• Barak, despite his fears, with encouragement of Deborah, stepped out in faith and defeated the Canaanites Jud 4:8,15.
• Samson, with all his weaknesses and human failings, when he acted in faith, was used by God to deliver Israel from the Philistines Jud 14:6,19; 15:14; 16:28

- Jephthah stepped out in faith, confident that God would maintain his promise if the people believed it. He defeated the Ammonites Jud 11:21,23,27,29
- From youth David learned to trust in God and became the great king and forerunner of Jesus Christ 1Sam 17:37; Rom 1:2,3
- Samuel learned from an early age to listen to God and respond becoming a great prophet, priest and judge 1Sam 3:7-10
- There were seventeen writing prophets as well as Moses, Samuel, Nathan, Elijah, Elisha and others who were used by God because they listened to his Word, believed and responded v32
- Many examples of people who acted in faith are found in the Bible, all of whom through faith achieved great results v33-38
- Countless others in subsequent generations have acted in faith, achieving God's will in their lives to this very day.

11:39,40 These were all commended for their faith Yet they did not see the fulfilment of the promise of the Messiah to whom they looked forward and who has now been revealed in Jesus. All of these people from the Old Testament will be included in the eternal kingdom of God because of their faith Lk 13:28.

We are encouraged by this list of faithful people who achieved great accomplishments by faith. This is the point of the passage – when we act in faith, believing what we have heard from God we can accomplish great things for the kingdom. We can do what they did if we know and have faith in the God they knew!

As we read and meditate on God's Word we become acquainted with each of the characters – they become our friends and they speak into our lives. We learn from them, from their successes and failures, how God dealt with them for good and bad. We learn to apply the principles of faith and avoid the temptations of life 1Cor 10:11-13.

12:1-5 The Race Marked Out for Us Life is a contest, a proving ground. We are surrounded in the grandstand by witnesses who have gone before.

Further priestly guidelines are given -
Let us throw off everything that hinders and the sin that so easily entangles v1 Athletes discard unnecessary hindrances. When we become entangled in the activities and thoughts of the world we loose sight of our first love.

Let us run with perseverance the race marked out for us v1 – everything worth having requires effort - God has set a path for each of us Ps 139:16. *Let us fix our eyes on Jesus v2* – our focus usually determines the direction we take Col 3:1-4. As we have been directed to follow the example of the past heroes of faith who looked forward to receiving the promises of God 11:13,39 so we must look to *Jesus the author and perfecter of our faith* who has also run his race. He struggled to the point of death v4.

12:6-13 **Discipline is necessary and beneficial** We must recognize trials and hardship are part of the discipline and training God uses in developing our character and perseverance to become the holy people he wants us to be v7. In fact difficulties are proof of our sonship and that he loves us v5,6. All great leaders and effective people come through the school of brokenness - Moses, Joseph, David. We accept and respect the discipline of physical fathers, how much more should we submit to our spiritual Father who trains us for our good that we may share his holiness! v9-11.

Faced with the constant pressure to give up our faith either due to persecution or the attraction of the world we have the need of perseverance to maintain our first love and avoid becoming lukewarm Rev 2:4; 3:16. Be vigilant, focused, determined in our commitment, removing obstacles and constantly applying the spiritual and practical principles of victorious living.

12:14-17 **Kingdom Conduct** As followers of Jesus we must make every effort to remain faithful to his commands –

• to live in peace with all people – we have been set free to live by the spirit of the law, acting with genuine love in all situations Jn 14:15; 1Cor 13:4-13.

• to be holy – we are now children of the Father and must expect to work with the Holy Spirit for the nature and character of God to be developed in our lives - w*ithout holiness no one can see the Lord v14;* Mt 5:48; Gal 5:22,23.

Many miss out on their calling or on the blessing because having responded to Jesus they are not prepared to follow him as Lord – Esau is an example of one who belonged to the family but lost his birthright through neglect Gen 27:37,38.

A KINGDOM THAT CANNOT BE SHAKEN

***12:18-24* Our glorious inheritance** We have assurance for the future. Without the revealed knowledge of God there is no basis for hope in life after death.

***12:18-21* We have not come as Israel did to -**

• the physical Mt Sinai, that could be touched, burning with fire, with darkness, gloom and storm v18 - with terrifying commands, that caused trembling with fear v19; Ex 19:17

• the people shrank from their priestly calling through unbelief and drew back from the Presence of God v19; Ex 20:18-21

• they had a temporal kingdom – a shadow of what was to come 8:8; 9:23,24 - they stood outside the curtain – the veil of the Holy of Holies 9:6-9

• they did not reach their potential and died over forty years in the wilderness Ex 19:5,6.

***12:22-24* We have come to -**

• the spiritual Mt Zion, to the heavenly Jerusalem, to the city of the living God - the dwelling place of God Ps 132:13; Rev 21:2

• thousands of joyful angels around God's Throne Rev 5:11

• the church of the Firstborn, whose names are written in heaven - there is only one body of believers, in the physical and spirit realm - each believer is a member Eph 4:4

• God the judge who is over all men - this judge is the one who brought us salvation, our advocate, with whom we will dwell forever Rev 21:3

• the spirits of righteous men made perfect - righteous by faith, made perfect by sanctification, complete when we meet Jesus 1Cor 15:49; Phil 3:21

• Jesus the mediator of the New Covenant, who shed his blood for us that we might live with him Jn 14:1-4

• a universal, eternal kingdom – the fulfillment of the promise 9:25-28; Rev 4:9,10

• our appointment as a royal priesthood 1Pet 2:9

• we have confidence to enter the Most Holy Place, by the blood of Jesus 10:19.

We are already partakers of these glorious promises By faith we can behold this vision of the future. Even as we are able to 'see' Jesus 2:9 and 'fix our thoughts' on him 3:1 we can see 'in the spirit' the vision of our expectation of the things to which we press forward Rev 1:10; 4:2. We even live in this environment by faith as we walk in the heavenly realms Eph 2:6. This is great motivation! Col 3:1-4; 15-17.

12:25-29 **We are already a holy nation**, a royal priesthood and a people belonging to God 1Pet 2:9. We must respond to the voice that speaks today and proclaim the message of salvation through faith in Jesus Christ v25.

Let us be thankful v28 – we express thankfulness to God for who he is - this is the atmosphere in which the Holy Spirit operates 1Thes 5:16-19.

13:1-7 **Fifth Admonition** Continue with sound practices of hospitality, kindness, generosity and moral living. We see that all the promises of God in the Old Testament continue to apply Deu 31:6; Ps 118:6,7; 2Cor 1:20.

13:8 **Basis of faith** - Jesus Christ, the eternal Son of God is the same yesterday and today and forever - we can trust him and the promises of the Word.

13:9,10 **Hold to the teaching of the Gospel** God's plan of redemption for mankind has been fulfilled completely in the life of Jesus Christ.

13:11-13 Let us go to him - bearing the disgrace he bore As the bodies of the animal sacrifices were burned outside the camp so Jesus was crucified outside the city wall of Jerusalem v11 – we must be prepared to bear the criticism and rejection of the world as we seek to associate with him and to live for him.

13:14 **The City to come** The philosophy of the world would tell us that the physical world is all we have, that we are material beings, an integral part of nature and there is no existence beyond the physical – there is no expectation of life beyond death. Scripture teaches us that eternal life is available through faith in Jesus Christ. We are to give our best effort to living in this life, recognising that it is only transitory and in preparation for the eternal city to come 12:28.

13:15-19 Let us continually offer to God a sacrifice of praise – the fruit of lips that confess his name This is the reasonable response to God for all he has done for us Rom 12:1,2.

13:20-25 We may be sure that the God of peace will fulfill his purpose in each of our lives giving us the power to do everything he requires.

Our Superior Person - Hebrews

The Old – A Shadow	The New – The Fulfillment
The Prophets – they were human 1:1 - they spoke on behalf of God - they spoke as they were led by God.	**Jesus Christ** – Son of God, has equality with God 1:2,3 - Heir of all things, Creator and Sustainer of all things - He paid for our sins and is enthroned in heaven.
The Angels 1:4-14 - they are ministering spirits.	**Jesus** – He is worshiped by angels 1:4-14 - He has an eternal kingdom 1:8.
Man – all things will be subject to him 2:5-8 - all things are not yet subject to him 2:8	**Jesus** - all things are subject to him 2:9 - He is now crowned with glory and honor Phil 2:9-11.
Moses - faithful in God's house 3:5.	**Jesus** - faithful as Son over God's house 3:6.
Joshua - they did not enter into God's rest 3:19.	**Jesus** - we do enter the rest of God 4:3; 4:9.
Aaron - appointed from among men 5:1-4 - offered gifts and sacrifices for sins.	**Jesus** – appointed by God to became the source of eternal salvation for all who obey him 5:5-10.
High Priest - 9:6-10 - entered the Most Holy Place once every year - offered sacrifices for himself and the people - offered sacrifices again and again 9:25 - only a temporal ministry 7:23; 9:24.	**Jesus** - 9:11-28 - entered the Most Holy Place once only 7:27 - sacrificed his own blood for many 9:28 - appeared once for all to do away with sin 9:26 - is after the eternal order of Melchizadek 7:24.

Person and Work of Jesus

The Book of Hebrews describes how Jesus met the requirements of the Old Covenant between God and the Hebrew people with significance for people of all nations and generations.

Eternal Son of God Jesus is the Son of God 1:2,5,6; Mt 26:63; Lk 1:31-33; Jn 19:7. He existed with God in eternity before the world was created 1:2,10-12; 13:8; Jn 1:1-3. He created the world with his Father & he now upholds it 1:3,10; Jn 5:17,18. The Son *is the radiance of God's glory and the exact representation of his being 1:3.*

The Incarnation He came into the world to be born in human form - he took on our humanity 2:11-14. He became flesh - he has two natures in one person - both eternal and human -
* fully human – it was necessary for the eternal Son of God to become human in the flesh to be a sinless sacrifice - *what is conceived in her is from the Holy Spirit Mt 1:20-23 - the virgin will be with child and will give birth to a son and they shall call him Immanuel, 'God with us' Mt 1:23*
* fully God – while Jesus emptied himself of his deity he retained the essential nature of God 2:9,10; Phil 2:5-8 - *the Word became flesh and dwelt among us Jn 1:14.*

He participated in human life so that we may partake of the eternal life of God 2:14,15 - how else could mankind obtain eternal life - *flesh gives birth to flesh, but the Spirit gives birth to spirit Jn 3:3-6; we are partakers of the divine nature 2Pet 1:4.*

His perfect life He lived as a human being in every way 2:17.

He chose a humble birth and lived as a man to set an example for us. He was *tempted in every way, just as we are – yet was without sin 4:15;* Lk 23:14; Mk 14:55; Jn 19:4,6.

He acted in perfect obedience to God, the Father 9:13; 10:6,7; Ps 40:6-8; Rom 5:19. His moral teaching over three and half years transformed society. He lived a sinless life and was condemned without fault 7:26-28; Lk 23:4,14; Jn 19:4,6.

His sacrificial death His death was necessary 2:9,10; Mt 20:18,19; Mk 14:36. It was voluntary 9:12-14 – he was always in complete control Jn 10:11,18; 19:10,11. His death required the shedding of blood to obtain forgiveness of sin 9:22; Lev 17;11.

He was crucified to pay the penalty for our sins 1:3; *he sacrificed for their sins once for all when he offered himself 7:27; to do away with sin by the sacrifice of himself 9:26;* Jn 3:16. By his death we are sanctified - *by one sacrifice he has made perfect forever those who are being made holy 10:14:* 9:14; 10:10.

He made atonement for sins. There was no other way to satisfy God's righteous nature and mercy, his justice and love, to account for God's holiness and mankind's rebellion, to remove the offence to God of denial and disobedience 2:17. Atonement must be seen from God's side Rom 5:11
• Expiation – to make up for - Jesus paid the penalty of sin, satisfying the just demands of the Law, God's moral nature Rom 3:25,26; 2Cor 5:21
• Propitiation – to make favorable, by removing the offense of sin to God 1Jn 2:2; 4:10.

He died as a ransom to set us free 9:16; Mt 28:28. He obtained eternal redemption 9:12; 1Tim 2:6; 1Pet 1:19. By his death the power of death and sin have been destroyed and the believer is set free 2:14,15. We have been reconciled to God – *we have confidence to enter 10:19-22;* 2Cor 5:19.

His resurrection He was raised again from the grave to vindicate his claim to forgive sin and grant eternal life - *this man, after he had offered one sacrifice for sins forever, sat down on the right hand of God 10:12;* Acts 2:24; 13:37-39; Rom 1:4; 4:25; 1Cor 15:17-20.

The resurrection was God's acceptance of the sacrifice of Jesus for forgiveness and salvation – *he brought back from the dead our Lord Jesus 13:20,21 - he became the source of eternal salvation for all who obey him 5:9; 9:27,28.* It was also confirmation of the statements, work and teaching of Jesus.

His ascension *He ascended into heaven and is now at the right hand of God 1:3; now crowned with glory and honor because he suffered death 2:9; sat down at the right hand of the throne of the majesty in heaven 8:1;* 10:12; Phil 2:9-11.

Savior He is the Lord Jesus Christ, the Messiah 3:1; 10:10; 13:20,21; Lk 2:1. As a result of his perfect life and death the one who puts faith in Jesus, God forgives all their sins & gives them eternal life – 3:1; 5:8-10; 9:12,15 ; 10:18; Jn 3:16. We are born again, adopted into the family of God 2:10-13; 12:7; Jn 1:12,13.

We are partakers of the divine nature 10:14; 12:10; 2Pet 1:4.

We have access to the Father 4:1-16. He has brought us back into a permanent relationship with God & we can now pray openly to God 10:19-22. He set the path for us to follow 12:2,3.

The Unique Messiah - Prophet, Priest and King All the prophets foretold the Messiah who will reign *with justice and righteousness Is 9:6,7;* 12:1-6; Deu 18:15-19; Jer 23:5,6; 33:14-17; Ezk 34:23-31; Dan 7:13,14. The prophet was required to provide wisdom for the people to live their lives. The priest was a mediator to represent before God. The king was appointed to govern and defend the people.

These leaders have been required due to the inadequacy of human nature and inability of people to live together without conflict, extremes of opinion and diverse moral values. Leaders have generally failed to act on behalf of the people due to corruption, domination, suppression and self-interest. They have failed to change the people - proving the need for a Messiah.

Jesus is the Messiah - our prophet, priest & king – he combines all three roles 1:1,2,8,9; 9:11; Lk 24:25-27,44,45.

• **Prophet** – He has given a personal revelation of God and the truth about salvation 1:1-3; Mt 11:27. He fulfills the Law and Prophetic teaching that went before 10:12; Is 53:3-5

• **Priest** – He brings us to God 7:24,25. He is our Priest and High priest 2:17; 4:14,15; 9:11; 10:19-22 - after the eternal order of Melchizedek 5:6-10; 6:20; 7:1-28; Gen 14:18-20.

He became a sacrifice for us, a substitute, all sufficient, once for all 2:9; 7:27; 9:27; 10:14. He is the sacrificial Lamb who takes away the sin of the world Jn 1:29. He made a new eternal covenant 8:6-13; 9:15; 12:24; 13:20; Mt 26:26-28.

• **King** –All authority has been given to him 1:8,9,13; Jn 18:37; Rev 19:16. He will come again as King of kings and Lord of lords 10:13; Mt 26:63-65; Phil 2:9-11. He will judge those who have not received him as their Savior & Lord 1:8; 9:27,28.

He will rule with justice & equity forever 12:22; 1Cor 15:24.

The significance of this recognition relates to the fact that God is declared as Lord, king and judge Is 33:22; 43:15; 44:6; 45:23.

What will you do with Jesus? Mt 27:22; Mk 15:12.

James

Introduction – James was a younger half-brother of Jesus Mk 6:3; Gal 1:19. He became leader of the church in Jerusalem. This is a pastoral letter and one of the earliest documents revealing the attachment in the early church to the Jewish traditions 1:1. It was difficult for Jewish believers to let go of the rituals and strict adherence to the law for self-justification. It was only shortly after this that the Great Council of Jerusalem was held AD 50 when the matter of salvation by grace through faith in Christ alone, without the need to observe Jewish customs was agreed by Apostolic Declaration. James was head of the Council Acts 15:13-35; 21:18. He came to support the decision after the report of Barnabas and Paul of the conversion of Gentiles and based on the Word of God – that all nations will bear God's name Amos 9:11,12. He was martyred by stoning to death at the direction of the high priest in Jerusalem for refusing to deny his faith in Jesus in AD 62.

Author – James brother of Jesus – written around AD 48 to the church at large.

Period – The Christian teaching and exuberant preaching about grace and justification by believing in Jesus caused some to ignore the law and depart from godly living Acts 2:38,39; 4:12; 13:38,39. James sought to show people that what they believed will be reflected in their actions. He was known as James the Just because of his virtuous lifestyle.

Theme – Faith Produces Response Practical instructions are given on the lifestyle that will accompany the outworking of genuine faith. Today many still confess faith without response.

A whole range of activities are covered. All of these issues were also addressed by Paul and are relevant today.

The main principles of faith are outlined -
*   Salvation by Faith in Christ alone – the new birth is by God's grace alone 1:18; Rom 1:17; 3:22
*   Response to God's Grace – action follows in response to grace 1:22; Rom 12:1,2
*   A changed life is revealed in obedience to Jesus - *Show me your faith without deeds and I will show you my faith by what I do 2:18;* Rom 13:14; 15:14.

Faith and deeds Some have seen conflict between 'justification by faith alone' and the teaching of James about the requirement for deeds or good works. For those who have experienced God's grace through Christ there is no dispute. They know the response of wanting to be like Jesus and to serve him, not out of compulsion or to obtain salvation, but out of love and thankfulness for God's unspeakable gift! It is the perfect law of freedom 1:25. The early church defined a Christian as one who 'through the knowledge and teaching of Christ, excels in self-discipline and righteousness, in firmness of purpose and manly courage and in an acknowledged devotion to the one, sole, God over all – Eusebius AD 325'.

Pursuit of godliness Paul's teaching to obey Jesus refutes the claim that he disregarded the law. The instruction to the believers in the Epistles to the Corinthians confirms the moral ethic introduced by Jesus and adopted by the early believers. It also demonstrates that Paul enforced this standard of conduct as a consequence of salvation by faith in Christ alone.

It is not about what one does but rather who one is becoming – an imitator of God! Eph 4:1-3; 22-24; 5:1.

This is in complete agreement with the teaching of James. Paul saw that the believer was released from the burden of the law in order to live a godly life by following Christ 2Cor 3:16-18; 1Tim 6:11; Tit 1:1; 2:12. Jesus came to fulfill the law by explaining the spirit of the law Mt 5:17.

SUMMARY
The Testing of Our Faith 1:1 - 18
Kingdom Conduct 1:19 to 3:18
Submit Yourself to God 4:1 to 5:12
The Prayer of Faith 5:13-5:20

THE TESTING OF OUR FAITH
1:1 Servant of God and of the Lord Jesus Christ Initially James and his brothers had difficulty with the claims of Jesus during his ministry Mk 3:31-35; Jn 7:5. After the shock of the resurrection James came to recognize the deity of Jesus becoming a follower and recognized authority in the church as did his brother Jude 1Cor 15:7. The brothers were present at Pentecost and were numbered at the first meeting of the early church Acts 1:14. Their transformation is further confirmation of the resurrection Acts 1:3.

James received a specific appearance of Jesus no doubt to assign him the task of leadership in Jerusalem 1Cor 15:7.

James saw himself as a servant, recognizing the Lordship of Jesus, as did the other disciples Rom 1:1; 2Pet 1:1; Jude 1:1. This is the model for all who follow Jesus Mt 20:24-26. James also demonstrated humility for he was head of the Council with full authority of the church 4:7-10; Acts 15:19,22-24.

To the Twelve Tribes Initially many in the early church saw the Gospel as being expressly for the people of Israel Acts 11:18. This was the early instruction of Jesus Mt 10:5,6 - as God's chosen people of the Old Covenant they were given the first opportunity to receive the Messiah. After the resurrection Jesus confirmed that God's plan of salvation was opened to all nations Jn 1:11; Mt 28:18-20.

Times of Trial – The early church suffered great persecution, initially from the Jewish leaders and then from society Acts 8:1; 14:2-6. James sought to encourage us to understand that there is purpose behind every event.

1:2-4 **The reason for trials and temptations** Faith must be tested to prove that it is genuine 1 Pet 1:7. So we can be joyful in trials for we know that God is developing our character. Testing develops perseverance which must continue until it results in maturity and completeness so we are ready for anything!

1:5 **We should ask for guidance** – God promises to give guidance generously in all areas of life - he will direct your path Pro 3:5-8.

1:6-8 **Believing Prayer** When we ask in prayer we must believe and not doubt or give up. If we have doubts we will be disqualified from an answer to our prayer. Doubt is lack of faith. A condition of answered prayer is -
- that we *must believe that God exists* - in all his glory and
- *that he rewards those who earnestly seek him Heb 11:6.*

Faith must be based on who God is and what he has promised, not on our circumstances or abilities. We must not be 'double-minded' - struggling between our circumstance and God's faithfulness. We believe in God - trust him through all situations with persevering prayer and we will receive his blessing v5. In this way our faith will be proven to be genuine and we will know God's blessing. We will also bring glory and joy to the Lord.

This principle applies to all of God's promises. Faith must be based on 'single-minded' acceptance of who God is and belief without wavering v6-9.

1:9-12 **We are exalted in our position as believers in Christ** – this produces humility and modesty. It is a reversal of roles - the rich become humble and the poor become joyful - each because of what Christ has done for them.

The result of the testing of our faith is that we will be blessed and will receive the crown of eternal life from God – to live with him for eternity v12.

1:13-15 **Testing and Temptation** Although temptation is part of everyday testing we cannot accuse God for causing us to give in to it. God is perfect, holy and unchanging Mt 5:48; Heb 13:8.

Temptation is based on our evil desires Rom 7:21-24. So we must learn to ask God to lead us out of those areas where we know that we are weak before we are faced with them - we ought to confess before we sin, not after the event! Mt 6:13.

We must recognize what tempts us, where we are weak and resist it at the first sign. Then we can overcome it through faith. We must avoid situations and company where we know temptation may occur. We must not harbor unwholesome thoughts or activities - little lions become big lions and big lions kill 1Cor 10:13; 1Pet 5:8,9. Cain is an example where thoughts and feelings became evil plans and resulted in action - sin was lying at the door Gen 4:5-10.

1:16,17 **God is the source of all good** The absolute good and moral nature of God is revealed from the beginning Gen 1:31; Ex 34:5-7; Is 6:1-7; 57:15-16.

Every good and perfect gift - coming down from the Father - who does not change like shifting shadows v17. He is always for his people Ex 34:5-7. So we can be thankful in every situation for *we know that in all things God works for the good of those who love him Rom 8:28.* In the same way *Jesus Christ is the same yesterday and today and forever Heb 13:8.* As God is unchanging – so are all his promises Zep 3:5; 2Cor 1:20. We must keep the immutable nature of God in mind when reading the Old Testament.

1:18 He chose to give us birth through the Word of Truth The greatest gift of God is the new birth - Salvation by the grace of God through faith alone, to all who put their trust in Jesus as Savior and Lord v18; 2:1; Jn

1:12,13; 1Pet 1:23. This gift is the ultimate demonstration of the goodness of God.

KINGDOM CONDUCT – guidelines on how to act
1:19-21 **Conversation** Be quick to listen, slow to speak, slow to become angry. Get rid of moral filth so prevalent in society. Let your conduct and speech be directed by the Word of God.

1:22-25 **Respond to the Word of God** Many do not read God's Word. Those who do often do not let it impact their lives. We are told to be doers of the Word and not hearers only. Do not just listen, deceiving yourself - do what it says v22. Do not look in the mirror then forget what you saw v23,24. Appropriate the Word - embrace it, believe it, live by it and you will be changed progressively to be like Jesus Jn 8:32.

It is the perfect law of freedom v 25 that transforms our lives through changed hearts that respond to the Holy Spirit rather than struggling to apply formal rules Ezk 11:19.

1:26,27 **Action must support words** Keep control of your tongue. Look out for the needs of those less fortunate than yourself. Keep free from the pollution of the world.

2:1 **The Lord of Glory** The basis for all actions by the believer is the relationship with the glorious Lord Jesus Christ who obtained our salvation. His example, instruction and self-sacrifice are the motivation for our commitment to him.

2:1-8 **The Royal Law - Love your neighbor as yourself** Lev 19:18 Believers must show 'genuine love' that acts in kindness to all, regardless of position, without favoritism or partiality v1-4. We look for the worth in each person and promote their wellbeing v5. This fulfills the whole law toward others. Genuine love displays the nature of God and shows that God's character is developing in us - we are being made into the same image v8; 1Jn 3:2.

2:9-13 **We cannot choose how we will apply God's Law** - doing only things we like with the people we like. We cannot be righteous before God unless we fulfill all of the Law, all of the time. James explains why salvation cannot be achieved by doing good deeds.

Salvation through faith in Christ alone This is why the righteousness that comes by faith in Jesus from first to last is so important v10; Rom 1:17; 3:21-24.

We show mercy because God's mercy has triumphed over our judgment v13; Jn 13:34,35.

2:14-17 Genuine Faith If faith is genuine it will result in response v14. A profession of faith that brings about no response is no faith at all. To express belief in God proves nothing if it does not impact the way we live. Faith that saves produces life change. Faith expresses itself in love - this is your reasonable spiritual act of service Rom 12:1,2; Gal 5:6.

2:18,19 Good deeds alone will not save Many people give intellectual ascent to belief in God. They follow a self-centered religion - *having a form of godliness but denying its power 2Tim 3:5.* They are right in their own eyes but fail to acknowledge or honor God. Even demons believe in God and tremble v19.

2:20-25 Evidence of Faith *Abram believed the LORD and he credited it to him as righteousness Gen 15:6.* He was regarded by God as his friend because of his belief in what God said which resulted in response. Rahab was also saved because of her belief that produced action - she heard about the power of God and chose to be included v25; Jos 2:11,12. Their actions did not produce righteousness but were in response to the grace of God.

2:26 Faith without works is dead A body separated from a spirit is dead. In the same way expression of faith is of no use if it does not produce life change - the two go together. This is consistent with the teaching of Jesus Mt 5:48; 16:24; Jn 14:15.

3:1-12 Control of the Tongue Taking the role of a teacher involves great responsibility and should be exercised with humility and diligence. It is necessary to exercise control over horses and ships in order to provide direction. The tongue also needs to be controlled – it is like a fire that can do much damage. It corrupts the whole person if not constrained - both in the one who speaks and in the one who hears. It can be put to good use or bad use and what we say reflects the condition of the heart Mt 12:34.

3:13-18 Wisdom of God is true understanding and with it comes humility that promotes good relationships Pro 15:33. Earthly wisdom involves bitterness, envy, selfish ambition and boasting and brings disorder v14-16.

Godly wisdom *is pure; then peace-loving, considerate, submissive, full of mercy and good fruit, impartial and sincere v17.* God's wisdom incorporates the fruit of the Spirit and achieves God's purposes Gal 5:22-25. Jesus confirmed this - *by their fruit you will recognize them* Mt 7:20.

SUBMIT YOURSELF TO GOD

Knowledge of God The way to live a peaceful, prosperous life is to submit to God and to follow his ways which are best for us – as we develop in relationship with God we change (ref p35).

4:1-4 The Way of the World The reason for conflict around the world is individual self-interest and unrestrained human nature – people living primarily for themselves. Tribal, sectarian, political and religious differences predominate and lead to war. Leaders become corrupt and suppress the people. This inability to find peace has plagued the nations in all generations from the beginning and continues today.

People follow the way of the world. They turn away from God and throw off constraint Ps 2:1-3. As a result they come under the influence of the evil one without knowing it 1Cor 2:14; Eph 2:2. They are frustrated because they do not find fulfilment. They will not seek God who provides peace Ps 133:1-3. When they pray it is for the wrong motives - they want their personal desires met. It is people who follow this lifestyle that James is particularly addressing.

4:5,6 God gives Grace There is a way in which human nature can be changed – it is God's way, from the beginning. The Holy Spirit comes into the life of the born again believer and brings transformation 2Cor 3:18; 5:17. The Spirit wants us to focus on the love of God and his kingdom. He longs for us to yield to him so that he can fill us with his Presence and power. Even as believers we can stand in resistance to God's leading in our lives.

God opposes the proud but gives grace to the humble v6; Is 57:15. We don't understand this fact. The mighty God chooses to dwell with the humble Is57:15. Pride and self-centeredness bring one under the influence of the devil and his ways.

4:7-10 Submit to God When we turn to God and are sorry for our selfish ways the devil flees. God knows what is best for us in every circumstance - when we humble ourselves and seek his ways he will lift us up v10. He will direct our steps Ps 37:23.

***4:11-17* Living Humbly Before God** Our attitude will change – also our conduct and conversation Eph 5:21. We will do the good we know v17. Humility will replace pride and arrogance when we learn to walk in fellowship with the Lord in daily dependence on him as he intended.

***5:1-6* Justice, Mercy and Integrity** Our attitude to possessions must be one of gratitude and generosity. We should be frugal in our lifestyle and attentive to the needs of those less fortunate – not living extravagantly and careless of others. We must be fair and honest in all our dealings

***5:7-12* The Lord's Coming is Near** Jesus told us to be ready for his imminent return Mt 24:30,36,42,45; 25:13. This attitude of expectation is encouraged by the disciples 1Thes 2:19; 1Jn 2:18; Rev 16:15.

5:9-12 The Judge is standing at the door v8. Our lifestyle should be based on assurance and expectation that the Lord may return at any moment. We must be consistent in our conduct, patient in hardships, considerate of others and persevering in trials remembering the example of Job and knowing what the Lord finally brought about in his life, restoring him to prosperity v11; Job 42:10.

THE PRAYER OF FAITH – the power, purpose and privilege of prayer

5:13-14 We are assured that God answers prayer Mt 18:18-20; 1Jn 5:14,15. We can expect that all God's promises will be fulfilled in our lives including provision, direction, health and healing both in our own lives and in the lives of our family as we put our trust in the Lord.

***5:15-16* The prayer of faith** depends on our commitment to God and his Word. We must be open before God and confess sin. Then *the prayer of a righteous man is powerful and effective v16.*

***5:17,18* A pattern for the one who prays** Elijah is an example of commitment and answered prayer 1Kin 17 to 19.

He was one of two great miracle-working prophets (along with Moses). He was a prophet of fire and power! Yet he was an ordinary person without great preparation or training. He was in nature just like us with fears and inadequacies. It was God's idea to withhold the rain as a warning to evil king Ahab. This was communicated to Elijah through prayer and he went and told Ahab before the event. He then hid! 1Kin 17:1-3.

After three years Elijah heard again from God that the rain would return - he acted in faith by telling Ahab. He then prayed till the rain came! 1Kin 18:41-46.

What can we learn about prayer from Elijah?
• Elijah was an ordinary person just like us - if you feel inadequate you are qualified for God's service Zec 4:6
• He was a person who had a relationship with God - he heard from God through regular communication Jn 15:1-8
• He was prepared to step out in faith believing what God says
• He was committed to God and challenged the people around him to be faithful to their beliefs 1Kin 18:21 - the Lord is always searching for such people to work through them 2Chr 16:9
• He was persistent in prayer - praying till the answer came 1Kin 18:42,43
• He never gave up, always ready to respond to God despite the circumstances 1Kin 19:19.
We too, must learn to pray always and never give up Lk 18:1-8.
We, like Elijah can do great things for God and be a blessing to others - if we respond to God in the same way that Elijah did.

5:19,20 Always persevere with those who are weak or led astray – the Lord is after the one in one hundred who is lost Mt 18:12-14.

Some guidelines for Prayer -
Approach - Jesus taught us how to pray – he gave us a model Matt 6:1-15 - the first five points involve worship and commitment Is 6:1-7.
Attitude – we need the right condition of mind - the conditions of the kingdom Mt 5:1-16 and the lifestyle of its members Eph 4:1-4.
Work with the Holy Spirit – who helps us in our weakness Rom 8:26,27.
Application Our Father wants the best for us Mt 6:32; 7:9-11. Be persistent - ask and keep on asking Mt 7:7-12; the shameless neighbor Lk 11:5-13; the persistent widow and the unjust judge Lk 18:1-8.
Authority We have the command and the authority of God 1Tim 2:14 - *By me kings reign Prov 8:15-16; He reduces the rulers of this world to nothing Is 40:23; The Most High is sovereign over the kingdoms of men and gives them to anyone he wishes and sets over them the lowliest of men Dan 4:17; Ask the Lord of the harvest to send out workers Mt 9:38.*

Knowledge of God Jas 4:1-10

The relevance of knowing God is emphasized throughout the Bible. We come to know about God in a number of ways. There are logical reasons which come from natural revelation and taken together give an understanding of the existence of God.

1. Ontological reason – the study of the nature of being

Reason perceives the concept of a perfect Being, who is absolute good, supreme, free from limitations – a Being of which nothing greater can be perceived. This Being is personal and chooses to reveal himself to mankind, in the universe. This Being must exist to attain to perfection. The beauty, complexity and vastness of the creation to reflect the glory of this Being is evidence of this perfection Ps 19:1-4.

God has revealed himself in the Bible and in his Son, Jesus – *be perfect even as your Father is perfect Mt 5:48; Heb 1:1-3.*

God is personal as reinforced by the Trinity and God's plan of redemption for mankind. Knowledge of God opens up a whole new range of investigation – spiritual and eternal.

The alternative of natural science is a purely physical, material universe without reason and eternal oblivion.

2. Cosmological reason — the universe is not self-existing – it requires an independent source

• The physical universe requires a cause. Every contingent being has a cause - a reason for being. Science searches for the cause and explanation for all things in the universe. The universe is here so there must be an outside independent first cause

In the beginning God made heaven and earth Gen 1:1.

Who made God? God is revealed as eternal, self-existing Spirit Jn 3:16; 5:26 – the absolute first cause Is 14:26,27; 44:24.

• The universe is finite and has a beginning and end – physically, nothing comes out of nothing. There must be a source for the physical universe. Science has come to understand since the 1940's that the big bang model (a beginning and end) best describes the universe – from the observed expansion of the universe it has been determined by regression that there was a beginning out of nothing. This has been confirmed by an understanding of the chemical structure of the universe from the first element, hydrogen

The Scriptures have declared the finite nature of the universe from the very first records Gen 1:1; Job 38:4; Ps 33:6; 90:2; Pro 3:19; 8:23; Is 40:26; 42:5; 45:12,18; Jer 10:12; Jn 1:1-3; Acts 17:24.

• According to current understanding energy appeared at the first moment – the total energy in the universe. From this energy matter began to be formed as discovered in 1915 ($E = mc^2$) so that physical matter came from nothing. Scripture declares that God made heaven and earth out of nothing, ex nihilo, no pre-existing matter, but out of energy – *by faith we understand that the universe was formed at God's command, so that what is seen was not made out of what was visible Heb 11:3*

• Being physical the universe has an end. The stars have a finite life. This is confirmed by the second law of thermodynamics. Useful energy is being consumed. The principle of entropy shows that the universe is moving to a state of maximum disorder and no energy – a condition of heat death.

God has declared that he will bring all things physical to a conclusion and make all things new 2Pet 3:7; Rev 21:5.

3. Teleological reason – of design and purpose, that demand an intelligent Presence

• The universe required a unique, narrow, finely balanced life zone involving diameters, masses, distances, angles, eccentricities, rotational and orbital speeds of earth, moon and sun necessary to maintain the atmosphere, temperature, chemistry and water for the existence of life on earth Job 38:4-11

• There are some twenty seven cosmological constants which are fine-tuned in order to form the universe and maintain life, which were present at the first moment of existence (the singularity) – this demands that Someone set the parameters. These values cannot be predicted or derived from first principles, only determined by measurement

• The irreducible complexity of natural systems, the simplicity of basic laws, the practicality of design, the functionality of components from the microscopic to the cosmic, the regularity and beauty of the universe is better understood by an intelligent Creator than by blind, undirected chance or force

• Physical science and biological evolution seek to explain the functioning and development of the material world – they do not address the existence, the cause or purpose of the universe or of life. They do not exclude the creative power and Presence of God. The best natural explanations for the existence of the universe are philosophical and unproven (chance, big bounce, multi-universes, no boundary conditions) with no hope of life beyond death

• The occurrence of life from mindless atoms cannot be explained by natural means - only life produces life. The human being is God-breathed – with potential and opportunity for eternal life Gen 2:7; 3:22; Jn 3:16

• Natural laws to not make events happen – they describe how things behave. There is always a greater cause behind events that determines the laws, a superior intelligence. Science can give no explanation for the existence of the laws of the universe or their nature (except by non-intelligent chance!) Job 38:31-33

• It is standard engineering practice to utilize modified design in subsequent applications with development to increase functionality and optimize performance – this better explains the biological fossil record than random mutation and mindless natural selection.

4. Anthropological reason – study of the origin and development of humanity

• The universe must have the observed values of all physical quantities for life to have developed – it was designed for humans. The humanist sees the universe as required for mankind – it is seen because it exists - it has no purpose

• The nature of the human being requires a greater Presence. We have the attributes of personality, intelligence, creativity, rationality, emotion, morality and relationality – in finite, limited, form. We have the highest aspirations but may descend to the depths of depravity

• We are each made in the image of God for the purpose of knowing and relating to our Maker Mt 22:37-39; Acts 17:24-28. We have an awareness of God in danger and deepest despair in calling to God! Ecc 3:11.

5. Moral Order reason – the sense of right conduct

• There is an objective moral order – all people have a sense of right from wrong and a demand for justice especially for one's self. We recognize a perfect standard in the fact that no one is perfect! Under certain conditions human nature is unpredictable. There is the paradox of greatness and weakness, achievement and despair, hero and villain Mt 15:19. The common sense of guilt confirms the frailty and failure of human nature. Many values are general – theft, murder, incest, pedophilia, rape - *when Gentiles, who do not have the law, do by nature*

things required by the law, they are a law for themselves, - they show that the requirements of the law are written in their hearts Rom 2:14,15
• The materialist sees ethical relativism – culture determines moral standards. In a mixed society who defines the standard? People in all walks of life break the law and lie in self defense. With no absolute standard it is left to the individual to decide what is right and wrong. We see the consequence in corruption, crime, conflict and civil wars
• God's nature and character define the absolute standard as revealed in the Ten Commandments. Jesus confirmed this with his teaching and example which transformed and elevated the ethics of western society – the Sermon on the Mount Mt 5:1-16; love your neighbor as yourself Mt 22:36-40; humility and serving one another Mt 20:24-28; fruit of the Spirit Gal 5:19-23 replacing natural ways; be perfect even as your Father is perfect Mt 5:48. Sin is explained as falling short of God's standard and forgiveness is available through faith in Jesus Rom 3:23; 6:23.

6. Experiential Reason – the experience of believers
• Countless people have had spiritual experiences which have led to commitment to Jesus and a transformed life. These have ranged from visions to a sense of the Presence of God. Similar experiences are common throughout cultures and history. The Scriptures declare that there is a spiritual world (heavenly realms) and a force of evil. While spiritual experience confirms the reality of God, the force of evil is also revealed Eph 2:1-5; 1Cor 2:12. We must test the spirits, whether they are good or evil – are they beneficial and for the glory of God? 1Jn 4:1-3
• Response to the Spirit of God requires effort and commitment and leads to positive outcomes. This confirms a personal God who communicates with those who acknowledge him. In this way the promises of God in his Word are fulfilled including an abundant life Jn 10:10. Many will not listen with consequences Jer 6:19; 33:3
• The materialist sees such experience as an activity of the mind. Many people who pursue a material existence face futility and even suicide.

7. Biblical Reason – the revelation of the Bible
• The Bible is unique - it is the oldest consistent record of God's involvement with mankind. It was compiled over 1,500 years by forty authors as God revealed himself, his nature and character, through his dealing with people. There is a unified theme throughout which explains the reason for the creation of the universe, the earth and mankind - to enter into a relationship with God for eternity

- The Bible is the remarkable record of God's dealings with mankind from the beginning to the fulfillment of his plan of salvation in the coming of the Lord Jesus Christ
- The Bible was inspired by God - *all scripture is God-breathed 2Tim 3:16; men spoke from God as they were carried along by the Holy Spirit 2Pet 1:21.* It reveals many truths about God that could not be understood without this direct revelation
- Moral standards of the Bible are of the highest order and have been the backbone of western society since the days of Jesus. It is the world's best selling volume
- Because people do bad things does not mean God's ways are wrong but confirms they are right!
- There is no other philosophy known to mankind that provides assurance of eternal life 1Jn 5:11,12.

8. Christological Reason – the supreme physical, historical revelation
- The fact of the life, death and resurrection of Jesus is undeniable from the Bible record, from secular history and from the experience of the believer. This is true more so than of any other person of antiquity
- In three and a half years of ministry Jesus gave the greatest enduring legacy in the history of mankind transforming nations and the lives of millions of individuals
- There have been numerous attempts to dispute, deny and explain away the life of Jesus. This is understandable because of the extraordinary claims he made
- He came so that we might know the mind of God in a greater way Heb 1:1-3. He came to remove the offense of sin to God by paying the price and providing eternal life
- You can deny him, try to ignore him or recognize him as Savior and Lord of your life Jn 3:16-18.

9. Knowing God – the reality
Life is not just about knowledge of God but about a relationship with God. Existence is not just a way of life – in order to obtain eternal life one must have a relationship with Jesus – *I am the way and the truth and the life. No one comes to the Father except through me Jn 14:6.*

1 Peter

Introduction – Peter was òne of the twelve disciples of Jesus becoming an apostle and a leader of the church in Jerusalem. He wrote two pastoral letters to believers throughout Asia Minor which have universal application.

Peter was the most impetuous of the disciples - he had experienced the holiness of Jesus Lk 5:1-11, walked on water Mt 14:22-36, recognized Jesus as the Messiah Mt 16:13-20 and then denied him Mt 26:69-75 before coming to give his life to the service of his Lord 2Pet 1:1. The transformation in his life as a result of the resurrection of Jesus is evident Acts 4:12. He received a specific appearance of Jesus no doubt to assign him the task of spokesman for the early church, a role he took from the beginning Acts 2:14; 1Cor 15:5. Peter became the Apostle to the Jews while Paul became the Apostle to the Gentiles Rom 11:13; Gal 2:7-9. James took the leadership of the church in Jerusalem Acts 15:13,19. Peter was martyred possibly in Rome in AD 67.

Author – Peter, friend, disciple and apostle of Jesus.

Period – A letter to believers throughout Asia Minor 1:1 written around AD 65 when he was joined by Silas and Mark 5:12,13.

Theme – Born Again to Holy Living The believers were established but under persecution. The necessity for the testing of faith was explained and the means of growth outlined. They were encouraged based on the example of Jesus and the glory of their inheritance, both in this life and the life to come.

Prepare your minds for action Guidelines for holy living are given, befitting the high calling of God's elect.

SUMMARY
The Glory of Our Calling 1:1-12
A New Style of Life 1:13 to 2:12
Kingdom Conduct 2:13 to 4:19
Overcoming the Evil One 5:1-14

THE GLORY OF OUR CALLING

1:1,2 **Believers Are God's Elect** Salvation is completely dependent on God's grace, not of any act of man Eph 2:8,9 -

• we were chosen, elected by God - by his foreknowledge

- we are being sanctified by the ongoing work of the Holy Spirit – being made holy 1:15,16
- we are set apart and empowered for obedience in service to Jesus Christ.

Our obedience is motivated by Jesus whose blood was sprinkled for us v2 – this refers to the sacrifice of Jesus as the Lamb of God for the forgiving of our sins v19: Ex 29:16.

We see again the work of the Triune God – Father, Son and Holy Spirit in the election, salvation and sanctification of the soul.

***1:3-5* Our Living Hope** Praise and thanksgiving to God should always be our response to the knowledge of what God has done for us through faith in our Lord Jesus Christ -
- we have been born again into a living hope Jn 1:12,13
- we have an inheritance that can never perish, spoil or fade – our glorious eternal future is assured 1Thes 4:17
- we are shielded by God's power from evil and harm Ps 23:4.

***1:6-9* Genuine Faith** We find great joy in trials because -
- we know that our faith must be tried and tested in order to be proved genuine, like gold in the refiners fire
- it will result in praise, glory and honor when Jesus Christ is revealed, at his Second Coming.

The testing of faith is the meaning and purpose of every human life. Every trial is in preparation for the life to come. This exhortation and teaching on the purpose of suffering and response was consistent among the leaders 4:12-19; 2Cor 4:16-18; Heb 5:7-9; Jas 1:2-12.

Our resolve and perseverance in suffering is possible because of our relationship with Jesus -
- we have not seen him yet we love him 2Cor 8:9
- we do not see him now but we believe in him Jn 20:24-29
- as a result we are filled with an inexpressible and glorious joy Is 61:10; Jn 7:37-39. We have this joy because we are receiving the goal of our faith – the salvation of our souls Jn 14:6.

This joy and expectation is the experience of all who accept Jesus as Savior and Lord.

Do you know this joy? It is available to all who believe!

***1:10-12* Salvation for the Gentiles** This salvation concerning God's grace to the people of the world was foretold by the prophets v10; Is 2:2-4; 11:10; 49:6; Jer 16:19; Rom 15:8-12. They also foresaw that the Messiah would have to suffer and the glory that would follow Is 53:4-12. We experience what they and the angels longed to see v12 - salvation through faith in Christ alone for the Gentile and the Jew. Peter came to embrace this truth through the encounter with Cornelius and the agreement at the Great Council of Jerusalem Acts 11:11-18; 15:6-19.

A NEW STYLE OF LIFE – the sanctification of the believer

1:13-16 **A Holy Way of Life** – *just as he who called you is holy so be holy in all you do v15*. Holy means to be 'set apart, consecrated for God'. We have been released by the death of Christ from the burden of the law so that we may live lives that conform to the nature of God. The life of faith is not about doing things – there is nothing we need to do and nothing we could do to be more acceptable to God. Life is about who we are becoming – more like Jesus 2Cor 3:16-18. We expect to grow in holiness through the indwelling presence of the Holy Spirit as he produces the character of God in us – *Be holy because I am holy v16;* Lev 11:44; Mt 5:48; Eph 4:22-24; Heb 12:14.

1:17-21 **Redeemed** We are motivated to pursue holiness because we have been redeemed by the sacrifice of *the precious blood of Christ, a lamb without blemish or defect - chosen before the creation of the world v19,20.*

1:22-25 **Born Again** We have been *born again - through the living and enduring Word of God v23.* This describes the way in which the new birth takes place – through believing God's Word about salvation through faith in Jesus and receiving the Holy Spirit Lk 1:35; Jn 1:12,13. We must then work with the Holy Spirit to live purified lives as we are being purified by embracing the truth of God's Word. A holy life is possible because we have the divine nature in us - we are God's children. **The Precious Blood of Christ** 1:19 The teaching of the disciples was dominated by the sacrifice of Jesus for the forgiveness of sin. They came under the influence and Lordship of Christ, captivated by his Person, example and work – *the surpassing greatness of knowing Christ Eph 3;8; believers in our glorious Lord Jesus Christ Jas 2:1; you believe in him and are filled with inexpressible and glorious joy 1Pet 1:8; Jesus Christ the Righteous One. He is the atoning sacrifice for our sins 1Jn 2:1.* Those who come to know him will be similarly captivated.

2:1-3 **The Means of Growth** The example of new born babies

- they crave mother's milk - they have a hunger, a deep longing, an eager desire
- they develop a regular pattern - wake every four hours
- they do this in order to grow - they can't survive without it.

In the same way we must develop a craving for the Word of God on a daily basis – this is how we grow in the spiritual life. If we do not have this craving then ask for it Jas 1:5 - it is vital to our spiritual wellbeing and our effectiveness. Job treasured God's Word more than daily bread Job 23:12. David would not neglect God's Word Ps 119:16. As food is to the body so the Word of God is to the born again spirit Mt 4:4. May we never stop growing!

The Bible is the Book by which the church will come alive!

2:4-8 The Temple of God Jesus is the Living Stone, the Rock on which the church is being built v4 Dan 2:34,44; Mt 16:13-20. Each believer is a living stone who is built into a spiritual house (temple 1Cor 6:19) to offer praise, worship and service to God through Jesus v5. This building concept describes the intimacy of relationship that is available between Jesus and the believer Jn 15:1-8. It is a relationship that is also available with every other believer and should be exercised Eph 2:14-18. The stone rejected by the builders often becomes the precious cornerstone that is chosen to support the whole arch and building. The Messiah is represented in this way v6,7; Ps 118:22; Is 28:16. Though he was rejected by his own people he has become the means of salvation to all who accept him Jn 1:10-13. Those who reject him will fall v8.

2:9-12 The Royal Priesthood God's 'chosen people' Israel were called to be his priests to the nations Ex 19:4-6. Through disregard for God and his commandments they lost their calling Num 14:22,23; Ps 95:11.

As a result of the sacrifice of Jesus on the cross of Calvary those who repent of their sins and accept him as Savior and Lord are born again and receive God's calling to priesthood v5; Is 61:6 -
- *we are a chosen people - chosen before the creation of the world Eph 1:4*
- *we are a royal priesthood - a kingdom and priests to serve God Rev 5:10*
- *we are a holy nation - I will show myself holy through you before their eyes Ezk 36:23*
- *we are a people belonging to God - redeemed with the precious blood 1:19*
- *that we may declare the praises of him who called us out of darkness into his wonderful light v9,10.*

As priests we offer a sacrifice of dedicated lives filled with continual thanksgiving and praise v9 - this is our reasonable response and act of spiritual service Rom 12:1,2. We are strangers in the world – our home is with the Lord v11. We abstain from sinful ways and do good so that the people of the world may come to give glory to God v12; Mt 5:16.

Bringing many sons to glory Heb 2:5-13 It is hard to comprehend the incredible future God has planned for the born again believer, both in salvation and for eternity *no eye has seen, no ear has heard, no mind has conceived what God has prepared for those who love him 1Cor 6:3,4;* Rev 1:6; 5:9,10.

KINGDOM CONDUCT

2:13-20 **Submit to Authority** It is God's will that we submit to every authority and show respect for everyone. This includes those in positions of leadership and responsibility even if we are required to suffer.

2:21-25 **Jesus is our example** He suffered for a just cause – us! He committed no sin, no deceit was found in his mouth v21,22. He suffered on the *cross so that we might die to sins and live for righteousness – by his wounds you have been healed v24* – from sin and sickness. He is now the Shepherd and Overseer of our souls – in complete control of every circumstance - we can entrust ourselves to him v25. The tree refers to the cross where we were freed from the curse of the law, sin and death to live for righteousness v24; Gal 3:11-14.

3:1-7 **Conduct in the Home** We must honor our family members and fulfil our commitments, obligations and responsibilities before God Eph 5:21 to 6:9.

3:8-14 **Kingdom Conduct applies at all times** If we show the qualities of Jesus we will find unity and be a blessing to others (we were called to do it Nu 6:22-27). We must speak wholesome talk and be eager to do good – even if we have to suffer for it.

3:15-22 **In Your Hearts Set Apart Christ as Lord** When we recognize that Jesus is not only our Savior but our Lord we give him first place in our thoughts and activities – we act out of love and devotion for him v15. Always be ready to give an answer to everyone who asks about the hope we have with a clear conscience, even if we are persecuted. Christ died for sins once for all, the righteous for the unrighteous, to bring us to God – we must seek to serve others in the same way v18.

In the days of the flood when judgment came on mankind people were given every opportunity to repent. However it was only Noah and his family who accepted God's salvation by building and entering the Ark. In a similar way we are saved through baptism – not by the water, an outward sign, but by responding with a genuine life-submitting commitment to God and so we share in the resurrection of Jesus - *who has gone into heaven and is at God's right hand – with angels, authorities and powers in submission to him v22* – we will follow him!

3:19,20 Now is the day of Salvation Jesus declared his victory over sin and death in the spiritual realm. There is no indication of salvation after death for departed souls or spirits Mt 25:30,45,46. Now is the time of God's favor, now is the day of salvation Lk 16:27-31; 2Cor 6:2.

4:1,2 Alive to God We do not follow the ways of the world nor are we influenced by them, but rather live for and according to the will of God Rom 6:11-13.

4:3-6 Dead to God The people of the world will give account of their lives to the Judge in the Great Day of the Lord v5; Rev 6:17. Those who do not know Christ as Savior are dead to God – unresponsive, living for themselves Eph 2:1-5. That is why we must tell them about Jesus so that everyone may be judged now and come to life in the Spirit – by being born again v6.

4:7 The End of all things is Near Peter learned from Jesus to look forward to his second coming as imminent Mt 24:30,36,42,45; 25:13. We must live every day as if this may be the day!

4:7-19 Suffering for Jesus Because the end of all things is near we must be committed to living by kingdom conduct, loving each other deeply, using our God-given gifts for the benefit of others so that in all things God may be praised through Jesus. As believers we must avoid offence to the world. However if we suffer or are insulted because of our faith we can rejoice that we participate in the sufferings of Christ v13. Persevere in all suffering knowing that God is in control.

OVERCOMING THE EVIL ONE

5:1:5 Leadership Although he was an apostle 1:1 Peter addressed the leaders as a fellow elder - no sense of superiority v1. This is a sign of effective leadership - to engage with all levels on an equal footing. It removes barriers, enhances wellbeing and encourages contribution, commitment and motivation. If anointing must be forced it is not genuine.

We must take our example from Jesus, from the incarnation to the cross, prepared to serve for the sake of others. Jesus changed the culture of society and leadership forever. We will share in the glory to be revealed v1. The shepherd took responsibility for each member of the flock - they were each under his care. He would willingly commit himself for them, with special attention and effort for the one that was weak or lost. The good shepherd lay down his life for the sheep Jn 14:14,15.

We are all saved to serve and so should willingly give ourselves to others who we can help, with the shepherd's heart v2; Mt 20:26-28.

As we make ourselves available God will lead the people of his choice across our paths. Young people should also look to those older for guidance.

The attitude of superiority and pride is one of the major causes of division and discouragement through the ages v3.

We must act as good examples to others - as we act, so others will follow, for good and for bad - we reproduce after our kind! v3.

Every act of service will be recognised by the Chief Shepherd with the crown of glory that will never fade away v4.

5:5 The key to leadership Being found in appearance as a man Jesus humbled himself Phil 2:8. Humility is the quality that God honors Is 57:15. It is one of the most difficult skills to develop because it requires subjection of self and our total dependence on God. *All of you clothe yourselves with humility towards one another because 'God opposes the proud but give grace to the humble'v5,6.* We need to recognise this fact.

5:6-9 Overcoming the devil We are in continual conflict – spiritual warfare - with the forces of evil that would destroy our faith or make us ineffective in serving God Eph 6:12 -

• First line of defence is humility under God's mighty hand v6

• Then cast all our anxiety on him because he cares for us v7. This is possible as we believe God's promises Mt 6:25-34

• Be aware and alert to the schemes of the devil who really is seeking to devour – to destroy our faith and witness v8

• Resist him by standing firm in our relationship with Jesus and on the promises in God's Word v9.

This is all part of the process by which God makes us strong, firm and steadfast v10.

5:10,11 The God of all grace, who called you to his eternal glory in Christ v10 - this is our God and his invitation to us!

5:12-14 Greetings Silas was a fellow missionary with Paul Acts 15:40. Mark was also working with Paul. They are here working with Peter. Babylon may be code for Rome but is also symbolic of all evil cities especially in the end time Rev 18:1,2.

Peter in Rome

According to early Christian writers the disciples took the Gospel throughout the Roman world and led the first communities of believers. After Mark went to Cyprus with Barnabas in AD 50 he was reported in Alexandria, Egypt where he led the believers.

Following the Jerusalem council in AD 54 Peter left Jerusalem and ministered in central and north Asia Minor - Pontus, Galatia, Cappadocia, Asia and Bithynia 1Pet 1:1. He may have led the church at Antioch for a time in the late AD 50's.

There was no reference to Peter in Paul's letter to the Romans AD 57 or in his meetings in Rome Rom 1:7; 16:1-23; Acts 28:15-17. Mark worked with Paul in Rome during Paul's confinement together with Luke Phm 1:24. Peter is believed to have spend time in Rome after Paul's release where he possibly wrote the first Epistle of Peter. He was joined by Mark who acted as his assistant and interpreter. Mark compiled his Gospel around this time based on the preaching, teaching and experiences of Peter 1Pet 5:13. Peter was possibly in prison in Rome when he wrote the second epistle and is believed to have been martyred by crucifixion under Nero AD 67 2Pet 1:13,14.

The Gospel Message

For those who profess to follow the example of Peter and Paul it is hard to perceive the departure by many from the example, teaching and lifestyle of Jesus -

• the additions and distortions to the plain teaching that liberated people from the fear of death and judgment – *whoever lives and believes in me will never die Jn 11:25,26;* Mt 24:4,5

• the separation of people from direct access to God by intermediaries – *for there is one God and one mediator between God and man, the man Jesus Christ who gave himself as a ransom for all 1Tim 2:5;* Mt 23:8-12; Heb 10:19-22

- the pomp, ceremony, opulence and wealth, all of which was rejected by Jesus Mt 6:19; 8:20
- the authoritarian dominance and self-promotion of leaders Mt 23:5-7

- the persecution, murder and exclusion of fellow believers Mt 5:44.

The early disciples declared -

- the call to the individual to be born again to the certainty of eternal life 1:3-5, 23
- the encounter of a personal relationship directly with God the Father through Jesus Christ alone 1:17; 1Jn 1:3; Mat 6:9
- the appointment of each believer into a kingdom of priests to serve God and the Lord Jesus Christ 2:9
- the election and sanctification (sainthood) of all believers 1:1; Rom 1:7
- the call to be humble, gentle and kept free from being polluted by the world 5:1-4; Eph 4:1-3; Jas 1:27
- the Church is the body of Christ made up of all faithful believers who meet to serve God according to his Holy Word – *each member belongs to all the others Rom 12:4,5;* 1Cor 12:12,13
- Salvation is through personal faith in Christ alone and not through the mediation of any human agencies Acts 4:12
- the Word of God is sufficient for all matters of faith and is vital for the sanctification of the believer through regular reading and teaching 2Tim 3:15,16
- There is no more offering for sin – *Jesus sacrificed for their sins once for all when he offered himself 7:27; 9:27; by one sacrifice he has made perfect forever those who are being made holy 10:14.*

Jesus said *thus, by their fruit you will know them Mt 7:16,20.*

2 Peter

Introduction – This second pastoral letter from Peter has universal application. He was possibly imprisoned in Rome.
Author – Peter, friend, disciple and apostle of Jesus.
Period – To believers in the church in general around AD 65.
Theme – **Participating in the Divine Nature**.
The Word of God - Hold fast to the true faith as established by Jesus and as confirmed in the Word of God.
The return of Jesus - Guidance against false teaching especially about the Second Coming of Jesus.

ASSURANCE OF OUR SALVATION

1:1-4 **The Divine Nature** God has provided everything we need to live a life pleasing to him 2Tim 3:15-17 -
• through the indwelling Presence of the Holy Spirit his divine power has given everything we need for life and godliness - he produces the fruit of the Spirit in us Gal 5:22-25; Eph 1:13,14; Jas 3:13-18
• we have knowledge of God through the person of the Lord Jesus Christ and through the Word of God - we see God in Jesus and in the Word Heb 1:1-3
• we have God's very great and precious promises so that we participate in the divine nature and escape the corruption of the world Col 1:13,14
• it is not by our own efforts but by our working with the Holy Spirit within us - following his leading Eph 2:8,9.
Peter was bold to talk about the Divine Nature because he had experienced the dramatic transformation in his own life and circumstances. This encounter is available to all who will embrace it.

1:5-8 **More Like Jesus** The divine nature grows in us by faith to include goodness, knowledge, self-control, perseverance, godliness, kindness and love. As these qualities of God, the fruit of the Spirit, develop in our lives we become more effective and productive through our relationship with Jesus our Lord.

1:8,9 **The Adversary** While our salvation is sure it can be undermined by the devil. He will want us to be ineffective and unproductive both in our character and service. He will discourage us from witnessing.

***1:10,11* We will never fail** if we grow in these characteristic of God's nature. The result will be *a rich welcome into the eternal kingdom of our Lord and Savior Jesus Christ v11.*

THE IMPORTANCE OF SCRIPTURE

1:12-15 It is important to be regularly reminded of the basic principles of the Gospel as this message gives us life and is the means of bringing life to others. Peter may have been in prison in Rome at this time and aware that he may soon be martyred – believed to have occurred under Nero AD 67.

***1:16-18* The testimony of eyewitnesses** The Christian faith is not based on the ideas or opinions of philosophers. Peter was an eyewitness to the life, teaching, death, resurrection and ascension of Jesus. He was greatly impacted by the majesty of the person of Jesus. He was also a witness at the baptism of Jesus and the Transfiguration when the voice of God acknowledged his Son. He experienced the Majestic Glory – the Presence of God recognizing the work of his Son v17,18; Mt 3:17; 17:5,6. He was witness to the resurrection and the ascension which transformed his life Lk 24:51; Acts 4:33.

***1:19-21* The Foundation for Faith is the Word of God** As well as the testimony of the disciples we have the Bible which was inspired by God. It was 'God-breathed' - by the Holy Spirit, into those he chose to be authors v21; Heb 4:12,13. The Bible is the authority on all matters of faith and it will speak to all who will pay attention to it. God will breathe into us every time we open it with understanding. As we do the Morning Star will rise in our hearts more brightly each day as we look forward to his coming v16,19; Rev 2:28; 22:16.

***2:1-22* The Consequence of False Teaching** Many will follow false teaching that is prevalent in all generations Mt 24:4-5. False teachers are those who deny the Lord who brought them v1 – the core of all false teaching is to deny God who has redeemed mankind and Jesus Christ who died on the cross to achieve that redemption 1:1. Their teaching and way of living are from the human mind based on worldly pleasure and self-centered expression so prevalent today. Judgment is assured -

• God did not spare angels when they sinned but sent them to hell v4; Mt 25:41
• He did not spare the people in the days of Noah v5; Gen 6:5-8

- He condemned the cities of Sodom and Gomorrah and rescued Lot, a righteous man v6-8; Gen 19:12
- Balaam was rebuked by a donkey when he pursued greed and consequently lost his life v15,16; Nu 22:15-20; 31:7,8.

The Lord will *rescue the godly from trials and hold the unrighteous for the day of judgment v9.*

False teaching promises freedom but results in bondage, both in this world and eternally v10,19.

False teachers have no shame and entice people to leave the truth for ways that are more appealing to human nature v10-18. If they have known about salvation it would be better never to have known Christ than to turn one's back on him and become again entangled in the world v20,21.

THE DAY OF THE LORD

3:1-14 The message of the first disciples was based on the words of the prophets and the commands of Jesus v1,2 – the unsearchable riches of Christ Eph 3:8.

Jesus taught the disciples including Peter, the following facts about the Second Coming -
- there will be scoffers – following their own desires v3
- they will say life goes on since the beginning of creation v4
- they deliberately deny that the heavens came into being by the command of God v5; Heb 11:3
- they do not recognize that the earth was formed out of water and by water, the essential substance for life v5; Gen 1:6-10
- they deny or ignore God's warning through the Flood in the days of Noah v6
- they do not realize that by the same command of God the present heavens and earth are reserved for fire v7
- the day of judgment and destruction of ungodly will come v7
- the Lord is not slow in keeping his promise – with the Lord a day is like a thousand years and a thousand years are like a day - without time v8
- God is patient – *not wanting anyone to perish but everyone to come to repentance v9* - his invitation is open today
- the Day of the Lord will come like a thief – unexpected v10

- the heavens will disappear and the elements will melt (be dissolved) in the heat – by nuclear fission, as matter reverts to energy from which it came v10.

In keeping with God's promise we look forward to a new heaven and new earth, the home of righteousness Rev 21:1-4.

Because of these truths we make every effort to be spotless, blameless and at peace with God v14.

3:15-18 **The deep things of God** Peter made reference to the teaching of the 'apostle and dear brother Paul' who confirmed these facts in his letters 1Cor 15:24-27; 1Thes 5:1-5; 2Thes 2:1-12; 2Tim 4:1. He recognized that some things Paul taught were hard to understand (the deep things of God) and were open to distortion by false teachers. He confirmed his acceptance of the teaching of Paul as revealed in their common preaching in the Book of Acts. While we embrace the straightforward teaching of Peter we can delve into the deep truths as revealed to Paul.

The teaching and letters of the apostles were circulating at this time and were held in high esteem v16.

The Creation of all things 2Pet 3:3-7

The major objection to the existence of God by natural science -
- the existence of natural laws do not require God
- who made God? Who designed the designer?

Some of the major unanswered questions of science are -
- What caused the natural laws? How did they come about?
- What caused the unique conditions that were present in the first instant that allowed the universe to come into existence, to form and develop to produce intelligent life?
- What is the purpose of existence?

It is considered that Darwin provided another explanation for complex artifacts where design is thought to be not necessary – that is natural selection, gradual change over many generations.

Our inexplicably self-ordered natural world developed by working up gradually and plausibly from simplicity to otherwise improbable complexity. The butterfly wing, human eye and the mindless snowflake are quoted as examples. Natural selection is stated to be a fair contestant to replace God as watchmaker!

There is no equivalent theory for physics – the universe must be as it is because we are here! It occurred by spontaneous creation.

Moral order is proposed to have developed by the same natural process. Natural science and biological evolution do not address the issues of existence.

The Bible says people will deliberately deny that the heavens existed by the command of God v5; Heb 11:3.

God is Spirit Jn 4:24. He is the source of all things physical; providing the total energy from which matter originated Is 42:5; Eph 3:9; Rev 4:11. Yet he is excluded from the field of scientific investigation by definition (the study of the physical world).

The fact that Jesus appeared in human history is undeniable. He gave greater revelation of God and his plan for the salvation and future of mankind. He confirmed that plan by his life, death and resurrection.

The Human being is the pinnacle of God's creation, with an eternal future, in God's presence, or separated from it Mt 25:46; Jn 3:15. Jesus warned that the day of judgment and destruction of the ungodly (those who ignore God) will come v7; Mt 12:36.

The End of all things 2Pet 3:7-13
Science recognizes that the universe has a finite life with several options depending on the critical mass which is uncertain. If only visible matter exists the universe will go on expanding to zero temperature & energy, no motion – the heat death or big freeze, believed to be most likely. With sufficient mass expansion will slow & eventually be balanced by gravity – a lingering death. If there is too much mass the universe expansion will stall, collapse, heat up & compress to oblivion – the big crunch (reverse of the Big Bang) – believed to be unlikely. In all options the fate of the human being is oblivion.

The Bible says that Jesus will return before this to bring about the new order v10,13; Mt 24:29,30.

Heaven and earth will pass away v12; Mt 24:35. There will be new heavens and a new earth that will endure forever – *the home of righteousness v13;* Is 65:17-19; 66:22; Heb 12:26,27. This is confirmed by John in his vision – *earth and sky fled from his presence and there was no place for them* Rev 20:11; 21:1.

Seeing we are aware of these things we look forward to the Day of the Lord with thankfulness and awe v11,14; Mt 25:21; Heb 12:28.

1 John

Introduction – John was one of the twelve disciples of Jesus becoming an apostle and leader of the church in Jerusalem. He wrote three pastoral letters with application to the universal church. As elder statesman and likely last living of the original apostles he spoke with authority to the church.

John had the closest relationship with Jesus Jn 13:23-25. He was present at the crucifixion and was entrusted with the care of Mary, mother of Jesus. He was there to the very end, saw the spear thrust and the body taken down from the cross and so he could confirm all the details recorded in the other Gospels Jn 19:26,27,28-30,31-37,38-42. He was prominent with Peter in the early days of the Church Acts 3:1; 4:13,23.

Author – John, friend, disciple and apostle of Jesus.

Period – John moved from Jerusalem and became leader of the churches in Asia Minor. He was exiled to the island of Patmos around AD 90 towards the end of his life where he received the Revelation. It was probably shortly before this time that he wrote the three letters intended for believers throughout the world.

Theme – The Deity of Jesus That Jesus is the Son of God and Christ the Messiah is central to Christian belief. John was aware of errors that were coming into the teaching of the church so he set down the truth as he had learned and experienced it during his three and half years of personal encounter with Jesus and subsequently as he lived the life of an apostle. John came to believe after the shock of the crucifixion and resurrection when he arrived at the tomb of Jesus and found it empty - the reality and implications of the things Jesus taught came to dawn on him Jn 20:1-9.

This letter was written to reinforce his personal understanding of the Person, life and work of Jesus and to refute errors.

Relationship with Jesus He also emphasized the reality of fellowship with God, the Father and Jesus, for the believer.

His specific reason for writing is given, that – *you who believe in the name of the Son of God - may know that you have eternal life 5:11-13.*
Acceptance of Jesus shows itself in a life of love for God and others and in obedience to Jesus and the Word.

THE WORD OF LIFE

1:1-4 **The Person and Work of Jesus** Without introduction or greeting John starts with a declaration about Jesus, the Word of Life and the Gospel. A similar declaration is made in his Gospel.

That which was from the beginning v1 Jesus is the Word of Life and he was eternally with the Father. He came to reveal more fully the reality of eternal life and to make it possible for mankind to have eternal life through faith in him. This was the conclusion of John after he had -

- **heard Jesus** - he sat under the teaching of Jesus for three and a half years

- **seen Jesus with his own eyes** - he had been present at the healings, miracles, confrontations, the baptism and Transfiguration, at the cross, resurrection and ascension and at Pentecost when the Holy Spirit came

- **looked at him** - taking into consideration all that he saw take place

- **touched and embraced him** – he confirmed the physical reality of the Son of Man - proof to the skeptic that he was real Jn 20:24-31

- **so he proclaimed him** - Jesus as Son of God and Savior of the world. John made this strong proclamation on behalf of the many who bore witness to Jesus after the resurrection Acts 1:3.

Relationship with God John had experienced the physical encounter with Jesus having lived with him some three and half years. This compelled him to acknowledge the reality of Jesus and who he found him to be, up to the resurrection.

At Pentecost John came to appreciate the new relationship he had with Jesus through the coming of the Holy Spirit.

The purpose of this proclamation is that his readers may understand and encounter the relationship which was made available at Pentecost and is now available to all born again believers. This relationship is not only with other believers but is first and foremost with God the Father, Son and Holy Spirit v3.

This fellowship makes joy complete for believers and for the Trinity! v4. Do you know this fellowship?

Two great truths are here presented as confirmation -
• the historical fact of the life, death and resurrection of Jesus, by an eyewitness
• the undeniable personal experience of those who put their trust in him as Savior and Lord, by one who knew it.

The Word of God Jesus is the image and exact expression of God the Father Jn 1:1,2,14; Col 1:15-20. He is the means of salvation. To accept Jesus as Savior and Lord is to become born again. This takes place by the operation of the Holy Spirit on the authority of God's Word Jn 1:12,13; 3:1-8,16; 1Pet 1:23.

The Word of Life The Gospel message describes the way of gaining eternal life and living that life. So we may equate the Word of God with the Word of Life - compare the declaration at the start of John's Gospel Jn 1:1-14 with this letter 1Jn 1-4.

THE NEW LIFE OF THE BELIEVER

1:5-10 **Walking in the light of God's Word** To be born again means that we have entered a new spiritual eternal dimension of life - the heavenly realms where we live in Christ Jesus Eph 1:3,20; 2:6; Col 1:13. We walk as Jesus did 2:6.

Fellowship The relationship that is available to the born again believer as a result of the removal of the offense of sin to God and the new life in Christ is -
• between God the Father, Son and Holy Spirit and the believer
• between the believer and all believers who walk in the light
Jesus explained this fellowship as the vine and branches Jn 15:1-8. He prayed for this encounter in the High Priestly prayer *that all of them may be one, Father, just as you are in me and I am in you. May they also be in us Jn 17:20-23.* John experienced this fellowship when Jesus was on earth and then through the Holy Spirit following Pentecost. He wanted believers to understand and experience this fellowship with God and with all other believers.

Walking in the Light As we walk in the light we have fellowship with one another and the blood of Jesus cleanses us from all sin v7. The criteria for walking in the light are that the qualities and character of God be formed in us (ref p61).

The Problem of Sin We have all sinned - fallen short of God's nature v8. Sin separates from God both now and eternally Rom 3:10-12,23; 6:23. The world ignores the fact of sin as shown by the deterioration of morals and the attempt to redefine good. For this all people must answer to God 2Cor 5:10. Walking in the light includes living in conformity with the Word of God.

Confession and forgiveness However if we confess our sin to God, he will forgive us and purify us restoring us to fellowship in his Presence v9.

2:1-6 **Jesus is the Atoning Sacrifice** for the sins of all who acknowledge him v2. He has removed the offence to God of our sin and puts us right with God – righteous, in right standing. He speaks to the Father on our behalf.

When we obey God's Word his love is made complete in us. If sin does occur we must be quick to confess it – then Jesus will forgive us and cleanse us. If we say we live in him we respond by walking as Jesus did v3,6.

2:7-14 **Walking in the Light of God's Love** Walking in love is the key. Love is the standard of the Old and New Testament – to love God and to love our neighbor - as oneself Deu 6:5; Lev 19:18; Mt 22:37-40; Jn 13:34. This is the confirmation that we are born again - that we obey Jesus by loving God and others, as he loved us Eph 5:1,2 – then there is nothing to make us stumble v10. When we exercise this love God's Word lives in us and we overcome the devil.

2:15-17 **We live forever** The new life contrasts with love of the world. Three common areas identify love of the world –
* lust of the flesh – cravings of the sinful nature – things that feel good
* lust of the eyes – things that look good
* pride of life – things that promote our own self-centeredness.

Eve was challenged by the fruit – she saw that it was good for food, pleasing to the eye and desirable for gaining wisdom, independent of God's instruction - she took it and ate Gen 3:6.

Jesus was tempted to pursue personal needs, personal fame and the way of the world, independent of God's instruction - he said *man does not live on bread alone but on every word that comes from the mouth of God Mt 4:4.*

In similar ways we are tempted to put the needs and ways of the world before what God requires. The world and its desires pass away but the one who does the will of God lives forever v17.

2:18 **The Last Hour** Jesus told us to be ready for his imminent return Mt 24:30,36,42,45; 25:13. This attitude of expectation was encouraged by the disciples Rev 16:15.
• Paul spoke of expecting to still being alive when the Lord returned 1Thes 4:16-18; 5:1-3
• James advised that the Judge is standing at the door Jas 5:8,9
• Peter remembered that the day of the Lord will come like a thief 2Pet 3:8-10
• John considered he was living in the 'last hour' v18.
We must live in this same sense of anticipation.

2:19-23 **The antichrist** In the last days many will turn away from the truth of the Gospel and lead others astray v18. The antichrist is coming - many have already come. He is defined as the one who denies that Jesus is the Christ (Messiah, Anointed One from God). He also denies the Father and that Jesus is the Son of God v22; Rev 13:1,5,6. There are many antichrists today.

2:24-29 **God's anointing** When we respond to Jesus it is because we have God's anointing on us so we will not be led astray. If we remain in the Son (in relationship with him) we have eternal life v24. As we continue to remain in him we look forward to his coming with confidence.

WE ARE THE CHILDREN OF GOD

3:1 **How Great is the Love of God** The magnitude of God's love is revealed in the fact that he has made each one of us who believe, his child through faith! v1. He has poured out his love on us, in us, giving us abundant life, redemption and eternal life as his children Jn 10:10; Rom 5:5.

32,3 **We will be like him!** We do not know what we will be like in the new kingdom but we do know this – we will be like Jesus! 1Cor 15:49. This is motivation for walking in the light – living a holy life – living like Jesus now! v2,3.

3:4-10 **Who are the Children of God?** Belief in Jesus brings life change – we seek to live holy, godly lives – like Jesus now.
To continue in sin is to give in to the devil v4,8. Jesus came to take away our sin v5 and *to destroy the devil's work v8*. That work was to deceive mankind into denying God and choosing to live for one's own selfish interests rather than for God. The child of God persists in following Jesus

v3. We know we are a child of God when we turn away from sin – God's seed is in us through the Holy Spirit and motivates us to love and faith v9.

THE ROYAL LAW OF LOVE - the Nature of God

3:11-24 **The Rule of Love** was instituted by God from the beginning - it is his eternal nature. This love is defined – *Jesus Christ laid down his life for us v16*. Jesus gave his new commandment - *as I have loved you so you must love one another. By this all men will know that you are my disciples Jn 13:34,35*. This love of Jesus for us motivates us to love one another and be generous. God's love is outworked in us. When we live by this standard we have peace and confidence before God who knows our hearts. We receive from him anything we ask because we do what pleases him v19-24. Further aspects of God's love are described 1Cor 13:1-13.

4:1-6 **The Right Path of Life** Many say they know the truth. Just because teaching is appealing does not mean it is right. In the last days many will be deceived. We need to test spiritual claims and philosophies of life by this criterion - if it acknowledges that Jesus Christ has come in the flesh then we know it is from God v2. Is Jesus honored? Do not follow false teaching. Hold the truth. Overcome the devil *because the one who is in you is greater than the one who is in the world v4*.

THE ROYAL GIFT OF LOVE – God's love for us and in us

4:7-14 **God is Love** Not only does love come from God but **God IS love!** He is the absolute expression of love. Love is revealed completely in who he is and what he does. God is the personification of love. He is the source of all love.

The love of God is undeserved - there is nothing we could do to be worthy; it is unmerited - we could do nothing to earn it; it does not depend on the object, or on the response, but is totally based on the Source!

This is demonstrated by the fact that God sent his One and Only Son into the world that we might live through him – to be an atoning sacrifice for our sins v9,10. *God demonstrated his own love for us in this: while we were still sinners, Christ died for us Rom 5:8.* He has given us his Holy Spirit v13.

When we acknowledge that Jesus is the Son of God we are born again by the action of the Holy Spirit. Then God lives in us and we live in God! v15.

No other belief system or philosophy presents a God of love and compassion who runs to embrace the penitent believer as Jesus explained in the parable of the Prodigal Son Lk 15:11-32. Our Triune God offers redemption through Jesus by grace alone. All other beliefs are based on good deeds and human effort.

4:15-21 God Lives in Us We can't love effectively with our own human love which fluctuates and depends on circumstances, feelings and response. But when God comes to live in us we begin to love through his love dwelling in us and flowing out of us – we love others with God's love v15,16; Rom 5:5. In this way love is made complete in us! In this world we are like him. We love because he first loved us v19.

ETERNAL LIFE - THROUGH JESUS CHRIST

5:1 We are born again when we believe that Jesus is the Christ – we are born of God.

This is what sets our Gospel above all other man made religions, beliefs and philosophies of the world. Jesus revealed his deity by coming to earth, born of woman, living among us, a perfect life (they found no fault in him Lk 23:13-25) and dying for our sins. God the Father confirmed the deity of his Son and the forgiveness of our sins by raising him from the dead. There was no other way that the sins of each person could be atoned (the offense removed). To accept this is to be born again by the indwelling Presence of the Holy Spirit. To reject this truth is to remain separated from God for eternity. Each one of us must make this choice Jn 3:36.

5:2-5 To love God is to obey his commands We overcome the world and its ways by faith as we respond in love v3-5.

5:6-10 God's Testimony When we receive Jesus as Savior we accept God's testimony about his Son. The Holy Spirit testifies with our spirit that Jesus really is the Son of God Jn 1:32-34.

5:11,12 This is the testimony The testimony is the declaration that God has made about his Son Jesus Christ by his resurrection from the dead - *God has given us eternal life, and this life is in his son. He who has the Son has life; he who does not have the Son of God does not have life.*

This is the assurance that every person may have and the warning to those who choose not to believe.

5:13 The reason for writing – that we may know we have eternal life through believing in the name of the Son of God.

5:14,15 Commitment to Prayer With the Holy Spirit dwelling in us we have confidence that God hears us when we pray and we will receive what we have asked of him Jn 15:7,8; Rev 8:3-5.

5:16,17 Control of the evil one Because we have this avenue of prayer we must pray for those who do not believe in Jesus. God wants all people to be saved and come to knowledge of the truth 1Tim 2:1-4. Because of the power and completeness of the sacrifice of Jesus all sins can be forgiven and all people who put their faith in him will be saved Heb 9:27,28.

Blasphemy This sin, if not repented is beyond forgiveness - that is the sin of attributing the work of God and the Holy Spirit to the work of the devil v16; Mt 12:31,32; Lk 12:10. It is the Holy Spirit who convicts of sin and produces the new birth in the repentant sinner - so to deny his work in us and attribute it to the work of the devil is unforgivable Jn 16:7-11. Many have committed this error 2:22,23; 5:10.

5:18,19 Overcoming Sin We refrain from sin as we walk with and respond to the leading of the Holy Spirit - then the evil one cannot harm us.

Prevailing Prayer The world is under the control of the evil one v19. *The god of this age has blinded the minds of unbelievers so that they cannot see the light of the Gospel of the glory of Christ 2Cor 4:4.* It is with this knowledge that we persevere in our approach and in our prayer for the unsaved, especially loved ones and those whom God brings across our path.

5:20,21 The True God and Eternal Life John's conviction that Jesus is True God, One with the Father and the means and source of Eternal Life is reiterated. This truth comes to those who embrace Jesus as Savior and Lord.

Walking in the Light 1:5-7
Some requirements for walking in the light of God's Word –
- being open and honest Eph 4:25
- wanting to be devoted to one another Rom 12:9-12
- mutual acceptance, agreeing not to give or to take offense
- encouragement – spur to love and good deeds Heb 10:24,25

- looking for the best in the person - how to assist them to reach the next level of maturity Col 1:28,29
- saying things that edify, things that build up Eph 4:29
- do not let problems smolder Eph 4:26
- being completely humble - the absence of pride, preferring others better than self Eph 4:2; Phil 2:3
- being gentle, meek - strength under the control of Jesus Mt 11:29; Eph 4:2 - the absence of domination & self-promotion - parking the personality – it is about you, not me
- being patient - persevering in tribulation & prayer, never giving up on people or the task Eph 4:2
- bearing with others - longsuffering, tolerant, working for the good of another - to seek the highest good of others Eph 4:2
- being the servant of others Mt 20:25-28; Jn13:12-17
- showing the love of Jesus – as he loved us Jn 13:34,35; 1Cor 13:1-13; Eph 4:2
- striving to maintain the unity that the Spirit brings, with common focus on the task of extending the kingdom Eph 4:3
- pursuing harmony with God & others Eph 2:14-18; 4:3
- desiring to contribute, a genuine interest and eager to receive
- seeing Jesus in the other person – let them see Jesus in you
- applying the fruit of the Spirit Gal 5:22-26.

These qualities of relationship are also revealed in the Sermon on the Mount, the high Priestly Prayer and in the character of Jesus Mt 5:1-16; Jn 17:20,21; 2Cor 8:9.

Walking in the light is especially required of leaders who understand and teach these principles. One can only ponder the state of the church and nation if these principles had been applied. It is our task to promote them in ourselves and others.

Group Norms - When forming a small group it is good practice to set down the guidelines for conduct and to obtain consensus of the participants from the start. This is beneficial for any group.

2 John

Introduction – John wrote a pastoral letter prior to an expected visit. It addresses the importance of basic truth and avoiding heresy. The lady and children are likely a group of believers.
Author – John, friend, disciple and apostle of Jesus.
Period – A short letter before AD 90.
Theme – Encouragement to continue in the truth of the teaching of Jesus in both belief and conduct 1:14.

JESUS HAS COME IN THE FLESH

1:1-3 **The Father's Son** John reiterated the relationship of Jesus with God as the Father's Son. Truth lives in us for eternity.

1:4-6 **Walking in the truth** There are many philosophies and worldviews that seek our attention. John proclaimed the truth based on his personal encounter with Jesus and his subsequent experience as he lived the life of an apostle.
The Royal Law of Love The core value of the Gospel is that we love one another and this is demonstrated as we walk in obedience to the commands of Jesus v5,6; Jn 13:34,35; 14:15.

1:7 **Jesus has come in the flesh** A fundamental truth of the Gospel is the incarnation - that Jesus has come in the flesh – the eternal Son of God came to earth to further reveal God the Father and to die on the cross so that our sins might be forgiven. It was necessary that he took on human form to be truly God and truly man, two natures in one person. To deny this is to be a deceiver.
Deceivers Jesus warned that there would be many who distort the truth Mt 24:4,5. From the beginning of the church there have been attempts to change the message of Christ – from within and without. These attacks are part of the antichrist – the ultimate 'man of lawlessness' who will be manifest in the last days 2Thes 2:2,4; 1Jn 2:18,19; Rev 13:1.

1:8,9 **The Teaching of Christ** John was one who sat at the feet of Jesus as a disciple from the beginning of his ministry. He was therefore in a position to judge truth from false teaching. We need to concentrate on proclaiming the basic truths of the Gospel to present a common message to the world.

1:10-13 **Kingdom living** We are in the world but not of the world. We must keep our focus on kingdom truth and values and not be diverted by the ways of the world.

3 John

Introduction - John wrote a pastoral letter prior to an expected visit. It was a personal note to a leaders about a problem of disunity within the church. It has application for all believers.

Author – John, friend, disciple and apostle of Jesus.

Period – A short letter before AD 90.

Theme – Encouragement over a conflict in leadership.

Be faithful in what you are doing

1:1-4 **Walking in the truth** Gaius was a friend of John and a person of influence in a local church. John commended Gaius and those who were 'walking in the truth' 1Jn 1:4-6.

1:5-8 **Showing hospitality** They were acting in the right way, showing hospitality to believing visitors Heb 13:2. This was important because of the need to travel for communication, instruction, and teaching. It is also a gift of the Spirit Rom 12:13.

1:9,10 **Division in the body** Diotrephes was another influential person who would not accept John's authority. He was involved in gossip putting those who supported John out of the church v9.

Unity within the organization is vital. Disunity distracts from the vision and dilutes contribution.

Many disagreements are the result of aggressive or dominant personalities and resistance to authority. Personality conflicts occur due to controlling leaders or unruly attitudes. Pride and self-centeredness supersede the fruit of the Spirit Gal 5:22-24.

Jesus prayed for us that we might be one – *that all of them may be one, Father, just as you are in me and I am in you - so that the world may believe that you have sent me Jn 17:21*

Unity is brought by the Holy Spirit and we are commanded to make every effort to keep it. This is achieved by being completely humble and gentle, patient, bearing with one another in love and remaining focused on living and proclaiming the message of Jesus Eph 4:1-6. We have departed so far from the example and commandments of Jesus Jn 13:34,35; 14:15.

Submit to one another out of reverence to Christ Eph 5:21 – this principle transforms all relationships when practiced in all levels of authority and across divisions in the body of believers.

1:11-14 **Faithful in service** Gaius was encouraged to *be faithful in what you are doing.*

Jude

Introduction – Jude was a brother of James, born to Joseph and Mary after the birth of Jesus Mt 1:25; 13:55 but not an apostle 1:17. He could not accept the claims of Jesus at first but became a servant of Jesus after the impact of the resurrection 1:1; Jn 7:5.

Author – Jude, a half-brother of Jesus written around AD 60.

Period – Jude was compelled to write this pastoral letter because of false teaching which denied the deity of Jesus 1:3,4.

Theme – Persistence will result in glory False teachers were condemned and believers were encouraged to hold their faith as they are brought to eternal life.

CHRIST - OUR ONLY SOVEREIGN LORD

1:1-4 **A Transformed Life** Jude came to acknowledge the deity of Jesus. He was a younger half-brother of Jesus along with James, Joses and Simon Mt 15:55. The brothers struggled with the claims of Jesus Jn 7:5. However after the resurrection Jude, along with James, a future leader Acts 15:13-21 was compelled to become a follower and a recognized authority in the church. They were present at Pentecost and were numbered at the first meeting of the early church Acts 1:14. This transformation is further confirmation of the reality of the claims of Jesus -

- The historical Person and Work of Jesus v4
- The resurrection of Jesus Acts 1:14
- The deity of Jesus v1,4,21,24,25
- Our Lord Jesus Christ is the One who will bring you to eternal life v21

Whatever one may think about religion and life, it is the deity of Jesus, the historical Person and his resurrection from the dead as testified by many eyewitnesses that each of us must make a decision to accept or reject!

The strength of Jude's conviction about Jesus is clear. He condemned those who use God's patience and grace to live independent of him and *deny Jesus Christ our only Sovereign and Lord v4.*

This confirms the understanding of who Jesus is as revealed in the Bible compared with the opinions of the people and philosophies of the world.

1:5-11 **Examples of Righteous Judgment** –

- the people of Israel were delivered out of Egypt under Moses and saw the Red Sea parted but did not believe and died in the wilderness v5; Heb 3:16-19
- angels who knew God's Presence were cast out because they rebelled v6; Mt 25:41
- the people of Sodom and Gomorrah who practiced sexual immorality and perversion had the example of Lot but ignored it and were destroyed v7; Gen 19:12
- Cain knew the right way and was given every opportunity to respond to God but chose to go his own way and was expelled from God's Presence v11; Gen 4:6-8
- Balaam, a prophet, received instruction from God but chose to pursue financial gain and lost his life v11; Nu 22:15-20; 31:7,8
- Korah, a privileged Levite, crossed the Red Sea with Moses, received the Ten Commandments and saw the miracles yet still rebelled against God's leadership and was destroyed v11; Gen 4:13,14; Num 16:31-33; 31:7,8
- these serve as reminders of the punishment of eternal fire v7
- those who teach and practice evil under the pretence of good will suffer the same fate v11.

These examples are given to demonstrate the extent of the mercy of God in giving every opportunity for each individual to respond to him so that those who deny or reject him will be without excuse in the day of account v14,15; Rom 1:18-20.

_1:12,13_ Maintain Good Conduct Those who openly practice wrongdoing must be discouraged or they will lead others astray. They are like shepherds without food, clouds without rain, trees without fruit, waves with only froth, stars without location.

_1:14-16_ Second Coming of Jesus The patriarch Enoch, whose walk with God was so close that he did not see death, prophesied about the **Second Coming of Jesus** in judgment – this would have been around 2000 BC! v14; Gen 5:22-24.

How did Jude know about the prophecy of Enoch – was there a record? Actually this is a direct quote from 1Enoch 1:9! The Book of Enoch existed centuries before the birth of Christ. It was quoted by the early church leaders but was not included in the Canon of the Bible as it contains some teaching not supported by the other authorized Books.

Copies were uncovered in 1773 and fragments were included in the Dead Sea Scrolls.

Hammurabi, king of Babylon 1792-1749 BC left a stone monument with a written code of 282 laws!

1:17-23 The way to overcome Jesus foretold that in the last days people would deny God and follow their own selfish interests and desires v17, Mt 24:4,5. The way to be strong in our belief is through being built up in faith through the Word of God and prayer in the Holy Spirit - sensitive to his leading.

1:24,25 Doxology This statement of faith contains promises and worship which will lift the soul in the Presence of God -

• God is able to keep you from falling – in every circumstance of this life and the next

• God will present you without fault before his glorious Presence – to stand before the eternal God, without fault – will be great joy

• He is the only God, our Savior – he sent his Son Jesus Christ to accomplish our salvation

• to God be glory, majesty, power and authority

• Eternal life is provided through Jesus Christ our Lord - forever! Amen.

When I think that the immortal Creator of all things is so concerned for me that he did not spare his one and only Son but delivered him up to be crucified so that I could be delivered from my sin and from eternal separation and be made a son and heir of his eternal kingdom! How can I not respond to the God of Love?

The Book of Revelation

Introduction – John, brother of James was one of the first disciples. Because of his close friendship with Jesus he was known as the 'disciple the Lord loved' – he identified himself in Jn 13:23 and 20:8. He was a member of the inner core of disciples and a leader in the early church Mt 17:1; Acts 4:13; 8:14. Late in life he was exiled on the Island of Patmos where he received a vision of Jesus and recorded this great doctrinal Book.

Author – John, disciple and apostle recorded the revelation he received directly from Jesus Christ around AD 90. It was a time of intense persecution for believers during the reign of Roman Emperor Domitian AD 81-96.

Period - A prophetic overview of the Church both at the end of the first Century and leading up to the end time events of human history including the return of Jesus Christ.

Theme – The purpose of this series of visions from God is to -

• **declare the sovereignty of God** in bringing about his plan and purposes in the destiny of mankind

• **reaffirm the deity of Jesus as the Son of God** with equality within the triune Godhead – Father, Son and Holy Spirit

• **reveal the glory of Jesus** as he will appear when he comes again to reign as King of kings and Lord of lords

• **pronounce the ultimate triumph of good over evil** confirming the righteous, just and inevitable judgment of God on the nations and unbelieving people of the world - sin and rejection of God will not go unpunished

• **reaffirm that salvation is through Jesus Christ alone**

• **confirm the establishment of the kingdom of God** – the eternal dwelling place of God with man as foretold in the Old and New Testaments

• **vindicate the saints** - faithful believers in all generations

• **give hope to suffering believers** by assuring them that the end of the story is victorious!

The Bible begins with *'In the beginning God created'* Gen 1:1 and ends with *'Now the dwelling of God is with men and he will live with them!'* Rev 21:3. This revelation is of vital significance to all people as it identifies the purpose of the creation and the destiny of mankind.

Specific letters to each of the seven churches under John's leadership also have direct application to our time.

Special Features – The Revelation is apocalyptic (uncovering) because it is direct revelation from God foretelling events in the future and in the end time. It provides a summary of the work of Jesus to fulfil the purpose of creation and gives a glimpse of the dreadful events that occur at the end of the world.

The Progressive Story Line Each series of events progresses the storyline further towards **'the Great Day of the Lord'** and the punishment of the unrepentant, each adding depth and new insight to the message. This serves to demonstrate the mercy and patience of God in giving people every opportunity to repent 2 Pet 3:5-10. The main storyline is interspersed with **'inserts'** which describe in symbolic terms details of events and personalities that impact the narrative.

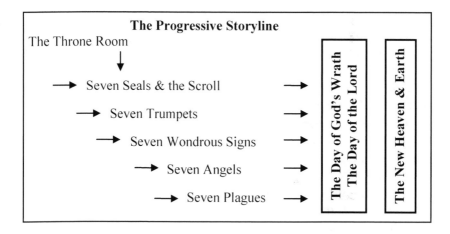

Some Guidelines - The message speaks about spiritual and eternal realities. Due to the limits of human experience symbols and pictures in physical terms are used in the same way that Jesus used parables. It can be understood by discerning people of every age and generation. It is necessary to look beyond the symbols to comprehend the meanings Pro 25:2.

The time sequence is not always chronological. It is sometimes repetitive to provide more detail 12:1-17, sometimes predictive to give assurance of the future outcome - this is shown through the Inserts 7:1-17; 14:1-5, 6-20.

The number seven is used frequently in the Bible as sacred, representing completeness, perfection. There are well over twenty groupings of seven in Revelation*.

While many things may not be clear it is important to embrace what is being revealed and appropriate it. Confirm what you decide with other Scriptures. Detailed study is worth the effort.

Why do we want to see the future? What we read must influence the present by encouraging and motivating us to tell others about Jesus and to work for the extension of his coming kingdom.

* Some groupings of seven - Churches 1:4; Spirits before the Throne 1:4; Statements about Jesus 1:4-6; Lampstands 1:12; Stars 1:16; Statements to each Church 2:1 to 3:22; Seals 5:1; Horns and eyes of the Lamb 5:5,6; Trumpets and Angels 8:6; Thunders 10:3; Wondrous Signs 12:1 to 15:1; Angels in the Harvest 14:6 to 15:1; Plagues and Angels 16:1-7; Heads and crowns of the dragon and the beast 12:3; 13:1; kings 17:10.

SUMMARY
A Vision of Christ 1:1-20
Letters to the Churches 2:2 to 3:22
A Vision of Heaven 4:1-11
The Sealed Book and the Lamb 5:1-14
The Seven Seals 6:1 to 8:5
The Seven Trumpets 8:6 to 11:19
Seven Wondrous Signs 12:1 to 14:5
Seven Angels 14:6-20
The Seven Plagues 15:1 to 16:21
The Fall of World Empire 17:1 to 18:24
The Triumph of Almighty God and the Lamb 19:1- 21
The Reign of Jesus 20:1-15
The New Heaven and the New Earth 21:1 to 22:20

1. A VISION OF CHRIST
1:1-3 The Revelation of Jesus Christ
• This message was presented in order to reveal something new about Jesus – 'uncovering something hidden'
• It was given to Jesus by God the Father with the purpose of revealing it to believers – what will soon take place
• It is not a closed message – it was meant to be understood
• It was sent to John who testified that he really saw the visions he wrote about.

There is blessing for those who read, hear and take it to heart. In fact there are seven blessings promised in this Book 1:3; 14:3; 16:15; 19:9; 20:6; 22:7,14. We are encouraged to live in expectation of the return of Jesus 16:15. The Book is called 'prophecy' seven times 1:3; 11:6; 19:10; 22:7,10,18,19.

1:4-6 **Seven Titles of Jesus** The message was recorded by John but came from the Triune God – Father, Son and Holy Spirit 2Cor 13:14 -
• Him who is, and who was, and who is to come 4:8; Ex 3:14; Deu 33:27
• The Seven Spirits (seven-fold Spirit) before his Throne 2:7; 4:5
There are seven statements referring to the work of Jesus -
• Christ – the Anointed One, Messiah foretold Deu 18:15-18
• Faithful witness – all he said as recorded in the Gospels is true
• Firstborn from the dead who rose again, believers will follow
• Prince of the kings of the earth, ruler in waiting, we will reign with him
• One who loved us – so much he died that we might live
• One who freed, loosed, washed us from our sins by his blood
• Who made us a kingdom and priests – to serve God!

1:7 **Look, He is Coming!** As the Gospels reveal salvation so the Revelation refers to judgment. Every eye will see him – including those who pierced and denied him. The first time he came to save – the second time will be to judge Is 2:19; Jude 1:14-16. This is a warning to unbelievers 6:15-17.

1:8 **I am the Alpha and Omega** The Second Coming of Jesus has the authority of the Almighty 1:8; 21:6. Jesus also has equality with the Father 22:12,13; Is 44:6; 46:10; 48:12; Phil 2:6 – the mystery of the Trinity.

1:9-11 **John was 'in the Spirit'** v10 We live naturally in the physical world - body (flesh) and senses. However God is Spirit Jn 3:5-8; 4:23,24. It is in the Spirit that we relate with him. When we are born again into the spiritual (heavenly) realm we learn to communicate **'in the Spirit'** Eph 2:6. We do this through prayer, reading God's Word, meditating, waiting on God Ps 37:4-7; 73:17 – spending time in the Presence of Jesus - where we take the time to be open to the Holy Spirit in us Jn 14:17.

On the Lord's Day v10 shows the reverence of the believers for the resurrection.

John was told to **write what you see and send it to the churches v11,19.**

1:12-20 **Jesus – As We Shall See Him** To this point what has been revealed was common knowledge. Now a new vision presents the Person of Jesus in grandeur - as we will see him.

The Vision of Jesus John saw the form of a man but could not recognize him -

- He was standing in the midst of the churches, represented as lampstands (seven – the number of perfection; lampstands required to shine with the light of the Holy Spirit).
- dressed in a robe and golden sash, representing royalty v13
- the Ancient of Days - symbolic of the Most High God v14; Dan 7:9,10; Mic 5:2
- all seeing eyes, feet of bronze, penetrating voice commanding attention v15
- the symbol of the saints in his hand v16; Jn 10:28
- He speaks the Word of God v16; Jn 1:1; Heb 4:12,13
- brilliant in appearance as the sun shining in full strength v16.

This is Jesus in the majesty of his 'coming again glory' to conquer, rule and to judge Dan 7:13,14. It is this symbolic vision of Jesus, as he really is that encourages and motivates us to serve him - it is at the core of the Book.

John fell down in shock! Nothing prepared him for this awesome image. **Do not be afraid** - the words of Jesus v17. The First and the Last! Again a confirmation of the position of Jesus in the Godhead 1:8. Risen, coming again to reign – with the keys of Hell and death v18; Mt 25:31-33; Mk 14:62.

Seven stars v16 represent believers, each required to shine for Jesus and each secure in his hand Mt 5:16; 13:42. Seven lampstands are symbolic of the Church (seven branched lampstand of the Tabernacle Ex 25:31,32).

2. LETTERS TO THE CHURCHES

2:1 to 3:22 There were more than seven churches in Asia Minor under John's leadership. The seven may have had district leadership roles. The letters were intended for wider circulation 2:7. They also have direct relevance to the universal Church of today! The choice of seven is both real and symbolic 1:4.

There is a common pattern to the letters – each has seven sections containing a greeting, a title, an assurance, a critique, a warning, an exhortation and a promise.

All **seven titles** apply to Jesus – all **seven promises** apply to the believer. In the same way, each section has relevance and application to the church and every believer today!

The seven critiques may be summarized –
* Communion – keep your first love relationship with the Lord!
* Conviction – hold on in the face of persecution!
* Conforming – avoid involvement in the ways of the world!
* Compromise – avoid drifting into the teaching of the world!
* Charasmarta – walk in the Spirit - moment by moment!
* Commitment – stick at the things you have been called to do!
* Complacent – don't loose enthusiasm – be HOT for Jesus!

Use the critiques regularly as a personal performance appraisal.

The **seven assurances** begin with 'I know...' Jesus knows exactly where you are; he is intimately involved in your struggles and progress.

The **seven exhortations** are common – *he who has an ear, let him hear what the Spirit says to the churches 2:7.* We must hear with the inner spiritual ear, the message to each of the churches - as it applies to oneself!
The final exhortation applies to all – *Here I am! I stand at the door and knock. If anyone hears my voice and opens the door I will come in and eat with him! 3:*20 - it is the door of your heart that you must open.

3. A VISION OF HEAVEN

4:1 **There is a door in heaven** – standing open. It was opened by Jesus. He invites us to come in. We can enter in the Spirit 1:9-11; Heb 10:19.

4:2-6 **The Glory of God on the Throne** There is ONE on the Throne, in splendour, a rainbow canopy of grace Gen 9:16.

He is sovereign over the universe, the source of all energy, power and activity in every situation v5; Is 45:7; Acts 17:24-28; Heb 1:3. All things in heaven and earth proceed according to his eternal plan and action Is 46:9-11.

The seven blazing lamps before the throne represent the Holy Spirit who sets the Church on fire – the sea shows the separateness of holiness v5,6.

4:4-8 **Then follows more new revelation -**
* **Twenty-four thrones** surround the Throne - **Representatives of the Redeemed** dressed in white with crowns of royalty – symbolic of redeemed mankind v4. The white represents salvation 7:13,14. These two groups, one from the Old Covenant representing Israel, the other from the New Covenant representing the born again believers, both seen as in the Presence of the Almighty, surrounding the Throne! v4. We must realize the importance of the first four thousand years of history (Adam

to John the Baptist Mt 11:11) when God dealt with his people Mt 19:28. The prominence and salvation of Israel in the last days is also foretold Rom 11:25-29.

This is confirmed by the Two Companies and the New City 7:4,9 and 21:12,14.

• **Four beings - Representing all Creatures** A lion, ox, eagle, man v6. God sees all things, everywhere present Ps 33:13-19.

4:8-11 **Worship of The Eternal Holy God -**
Day and night the four beings never stop crying -

> *Holy, holy, holy is the Lord God Almighty,*
> *who was, and is, and is to come v8*

They declare the Eternal Sovereign God who is holy.

Then the representatives of the redeemed of all generations fall down and lay their crowns before the Throne saying -

> *You are worthy our Lord and God, to receive glory and honor*
> *and power, for you created all things and by your will*
> *they were created and have their being! v10*

This anthem expounds the purpose of creation.

The throne of God is a place of worship in which we may join.

4. THE SEALED BOOK and THE LAMB

To this point there has been no mention of Jesus in heaven!

5:1-4 **The Scroll** The One on the Throne held a Scroll (sealed book) written on both sides, containing the future – the culmination of human history and God's plan for mankind - with Seven Seals. How could God's plan conclude without a way of salvation for the repentant believer?

There was no one worthy, who could earn the right to open it. To this point of time the offense of sin excluded all from the eternal Presence of God Rom 3:23; 6:23. No wonder John wept!

5:5-10 **The Glory of Jesus Christ** The Lion of Judah, the Root of David has triumphed and is able to open the Scroll and its Seven Seals v5. Jesus is worthy and no other, for he only, by his sinless sacrifice has fulfilled God's promise through the prophets of a Messiah of the line of Judah and to David for an eternal kingdom Gen 49:9,10; 2Sam 7:16.

He appeared as a *Lamb, looking as if it had been slain v6* – signifying his sacrificial death to forgive sin, conquer death and destroy evil. This was ordained from the creation of the world and fulfilled at Calvary. **The victory has already been won!** 11:15; 12:10,11; Jn 12:31; Col 2:14,15.

The Lamb was *standing in the 'centre of the throne'! v6* - the mystery of the Godhead. The seven horns represent complete power; seven eyes represent omniscience (all-seeing) of Jesus.
The Lamb took the scroll v7 – the culmination of human destiny could now proceed. Forgiveness and eternal life could be received by faith in Jesus alone!
Then began a mighty symphony of praise and worship.
The Song of the Redeemed As a result of this mighty act the representatives of all creatures and of the Redeemed fell down in adoration of Jesus – included in their worship are the prayers of the saints which are prominent before the Throne of God v8. They sing a new song –

You are worthy to take the scroll and to open its seals for you
were slain and with your blood you purchased men for God
from every tribe and language and people and nation
You have made them to be a kingdom and priests to
serve our God - And they will reign on the earth

The price has been paid, their position is secure – they are a kingdom and priests to serve our God - they will reign on earth v9-11; 2:26. This statement defines God's plan of creation and salvation for the people of the earth.

5:11-14 **The Father and the Son Worshiped** After revelation of the finished work of Jesus the angels and representatives of creation worship him -

Worthy is the Lamb who was slain
to receive power and wealth and wisdom and strength
And honor and glory and praise

Then all in heaven and on earth break out in giving the highest praise and adoration to both the Father and the Son!

To him who sits on the Throne and to the Lamb
be praise and honor and glory and power forever and ever!

This is testimony to the finished work of Jesus as the Messiah and also acknowledgement of the unity of the Trinity - Father, Son and Holy Spirit.

5. THE SEVEN SEALS – **progressing the future**
The future sealed up until now can proceed because the way of redemption has been made possible by Jesus - it unfolds by the sovereignty of God.

6:1-17 **The first series of events** As each seal was opened by the Lamb an event proceeded, resulting in progressive deterioration of moral, social and ecological conditions leading to the end of human history. Four horsemen given authority by God (forces set loose Ezk 14:21) to bring persecution and judgment. This course of events is the consequence of independence from God and unconstrained human nature. The first five events have unfolded since the return of Jesus to heaven. The sixth may be on us today.

First Seal – conquest by false religion, deceptive teaching and philosophy v1
Second Seal – takes away the ability to make peace from the earth v3
Third Seal – brings poverty in the midst of plenty v5, increasing separation
Fourth Seal – brings death by conflict, famine and plague v8
Fifth Seal – brings increasing persecution of believers v9
Sixth Seal – brings disturbance of the heavens, against world powers v12-16; Joel 1:15. Examples of these related events have occurred in the past - blackened sun, red moon, asteroids, comets, volcanoes, earthquakes -

    Then the Great Day of the Wrath of God v17; Is 13:6-11
The Day of the Lord has been foretold by the prophets Is 2:12; Zep 1:14. Each of these events – the Seals, Trumpets and Plagues lead up to this finale!

Jesus' Account of the Last Days
Jesus described this series of events in the week before the crucifixion when asked about the end time. While many of the events led up to the destruction of the Temple in AD 70 the teaching of Jesus in Mt 24:1-44 has great similarity and parallels with the six seals of Revelation (also Lk 21:8-19,25-28). This is common in mid and long term prophecy 12:5; Is 7:14; 9:6,7; Mt 1:23; 24:15; Dan 11:31; 12:11 -

Seal 1 - False teaching, many will be deceived v5 - multi-faith compromise
Seal 2 - Wars and threat of wars v6 - peace will be taken from the earth
Seal 3 - Poverty and plenty with national conflict v7 - nation rising up against nation, people against people, ethnic tribe against tribe
Seal 4 – Famine and earthquakes – the beginning of the end v7
Seal 5 – Persecution, hatred, falling away, increase of wickedness v9-12
Seal 6 – Immediately after those days heavenly disruption v29 -

    They will see the Son of Man coming on the clouds v30

The Great Day of God's Wrath and the Second Coming of Jesus are related. Before this Day of Reckoning believers will have been secured! 7:3; 13:8.

7:1-12 Two Companies – Insert 1 At this crucial point before God's Wrath is announced and poured out on unbelieving mankind the first insert is introduced. It describes two companies or groups who are foreseen in heaven. They have been sealed so their future is assured v3; Eph 1:13,14.

• **Israel** – faithful believers from the beginning in the Old Testament period are represented symbolically by twelve groups of 12,000 – God's relationship with them is significant v1-8. They include the Patriarchs and are saved because they believed God in faith Jer 31:36; Rom 4:13; Heb 11;1-40
• **The Great Multitude** – the second group are those who put their faith in Jesus represented as people from every tribe, tongue, people and nation v9.

These two groups represent believers of all generations 4:2-11 - they will not be harmed in the end time events. This is of great encouragement.

The redeemed cry out ***Salvation belongs to our God, who sits on the Throne, and to the Lamb v10.*** The glorious future of the believer is declared.

7:13-17 Their robes washed white in the blood of the Lamb Is 61:10 - their future is assured in the very Presence of God v15 - the Lamb will be their Shepherd for eternity v17; Ps 23:1-6; Jn 10:27,28.

8:1-5 The Place of Prayer A new revelation of the importance of prayer is given. With the opening of the **Seventh Seal** there is a brief silence – heaven pauses when the saints pray! An angel takes action v5. Our prayer is powerful and effective - it rises before the Presence of God and is taken into account in outworking the purposes of God 4:5; Jas 5:16-18. We, now, like John, may be 'in the Spirit' and enter the Throne room at any time in prayer and meditation because of the completed work of Jesus 4:1,2; Heb 10:19 - how often do we make use of this great privilege?

6. THE SEVEN TRUMPETS – announcing the end
8:6 to 9:21 The second series of events was ushered in by the opening of the **Seventh Seal.** Trumpets are used to announce an important event. Here they herald the beginnings of God's final judgment on the nations

and the end time! They are both warnings and judgment - there is still time to repent.

The heavenly disturbances of the Sixth Seal intensify with the first four Trumpets which impact the elements. They are followed by three more Trumpets with judgment against unbelievers, described as 'Woes' because of their dramatic effect on mankind. Believers will not be harmed, having been sealed 7:3 as in the case of Israel in the days of the plagues in Egypt who were sealed by the blood of the lamb on the door post - they were differentiated from Egypt Ex 8:22,23; 9:4; 10:22,23.

The description of these events is most plausible in view of our knowledge of the impact history of the surface of the earth, moon and other planets.

First Trumpet – against the land – hail and fire 8:7

Second Trumpet – against the sea – turned to blood 8:8

Third Trumpet – against the rivers – waters turned bitter 8:10

Fourth Trumpet – against the heavens - disturbances 8:12

Fifth Trumpet – **(the First Woe)** - torment of mankind by demonic forces (those not sealed) - they could not kill 9:1-12

Sixth Trumpet – **(the Second Woe)** a demonic army from the Euphrates is released to kill a third of mankind 9:13-19. This Woe continues to 11:14. Despite these calamities unbelievers who survive do not repent 9:20.

The Witness of the Saints Two more inserts describe the importance of witnessing which is crucial to the overall storyline.

10:1-11 **The Open Book – Insert 2** The little scroll represents the Gospel, open at present v2. The seven thunders represent the voice of prayer, multitudes never silent, for the unsaved and for the coming kingdom v3.

Mystery of God The Gospel contains God's plan to bring all things together under one head, even Christ v7; Eph 1:9,10. This message is sweet because of the assurance of salvation to those who accept it; bitter because of sorrow for those who reject it. It is also sweet to tell others but bitter because of hardship and persecution v9-11. The Gospel must be proclaimed on land and across the seas, around the world, until the end. **This is our present task** Mt 28:18-20. The time is short v6.

11:1-14 **Two Witnesses – Insert 3** There will be final brief testimony to the fallen world v2. The temple (sanctuary) represents the people of God on earth at the time. The city trampled by the world represents dominance by the world order. The final witnesses will be of the order of God's two great miracle-working prophets Moses and Elijah v6. **The Great City** represents the ultimate stand of evil against God - *figuratively called Sodom and Egypt* where Israel was enslaved and Jerusalem *where also their Lord was crucified v8;* 16:19; 17:5,18; 18:2,10. This last chance for salvation is relevant to the people of Israel Rom 11:25-27. Unrepentant mankind will be without excuse. The Two Witnesses are killed by antichrist - they come back to life and are raptured v12. This concludes the warning of the **Sixth Trumpet (the Second Woe)**. The **Third Woe** is coming soon (in time), but not till 15:1.

11:2,3 **God's Time Period for Judgment** The time period of 42 months v2 is referred to many times in prophecy. 42 months is used in 11:2 and 13:5 with 1,260 days in 11:3 and 12:6. Time, times and half a time is used in 12:14; Dan 7:25 and 12:7. These periods all equal three and a half years and are symbolic of a testing time for God's people 11:3,12;6,14. There is a limit on the extent of evil activities undertaken by the world 11:2; 13:5; Dan 7:25; 9:27; 12:7.

11:15-19 **Kingdom of God - The Seventh (last) Trumpet** sounds announcing the replacement of the kingdom of this world with the kingdom of God which is about to occur after the **third and final Woe** 16:1-21; 1Cor 15:52; 1Thes 4:16. This kingdom was foretold by the prophets and introduced by Jesus Is 9:6,7; Mk 1:14,15. In anticipation the heavenly host proclaim -

The kingdom of the world has become the kingdom of our Lord and of his Christ, and he will reign forever and ever v15

The representatives of the redeemed give thanks to God as he exerts his power in the punishment of evil and the realization of his eternal kingdom v17.

The time has come for judging the dead and for rewarding your servants the prophets and your saints v18

God's Great Covenant The plan of God from eternity has been to dwell with man. Heaven is opened and the action of God follows! v19.

7. SEVEN WONDROUS SIGNS - Earthly Conflict – Insert 4

An Overview of the History of Mankind Before describing the final end time conflict an overview is given of the seven important amazing events of human history from God's perspective.

12:1,2 **Wonder 1 – A Woman clothed with the Sun** The chosen people of God in the Old Testament including the nation of Israel.

12:3,4 **Wonder 2 – A Dragon** Satan empowering rulers of the world and the source of all evil – who sought to destroy the woman's child. He is *that ancient serpent called the devil - who leads the whole world astray 12:9* - the accuser and deceiver of mankind from the beginning 12:10; Gen 3:1. He is represented with 7 heads, 10 horns and 7 crowns v3; 17:8-14.

12:5,6 **Wonder 3 – A Child** Jesus was born out of the nation of Israel, of the tribe of Judah – he will rule the nations with an iron rod 19:15.

12:7-17 **War Against the Saints - the Church Age** The devil and his angelic supporters were cast out of heaven to earth v9 – this situation was associated with the victory of Jesus on the cross and the opening of salvation to the nations v10-12. The devil turned his attack on the offspring of the woman – the believers of the New Covenant v17 who overcome him by the blood of the Lamb and by the word of their testimony v11.

13:1-10 **Wonder 4 – The Beast out of the Sea** In the last days there will be a major outbreak of evil - **one world empire**, a secular universal government – a political union offering man-made prosperity, peace and plenty. It will be worse than all that went before - with 10 horns and 7 heads as on the dragon but 10 crowns v1 - incorporating all the evil features of past empires (leopard, bear and lion) having the power and authority of Satan v2 - the return of an evil leader v3, who will devour the whole earth v4, persecute the saints and overpower them v7; 17:8-14; Dan 7:1-8,11; Mt 4:8.

This has been the continual desire of mankind to achieve world domination and independence from God. It will reach culmination in the end time Gen 11:4-6. Believers must bear the persecution of the world systems and people as God's representatives to show that there are those who choose God's authority and ways despite the consequences v10. They will be vindicated in the end 12:11. We are progressing towards this sign!

This beast will be the final antichrist who stands opposed to or instead of Jesus - called the man of sin. He is the little horn Dan 7:8,24,25; 11:36 and the eighth king 17:9-11; 19:19. A dictator, his reign will be short v5; 11:3.

The personification of evil has occurred in all generations revealing the determination of the evil one to oppose and usurp the authority of God and overcome the faithful believer. It is manifest in -

- The desolation of the Temple by Antiochus in 167 BC Dan 8:1-27
- The destruction of the Temple by Titus in AD 70 Dan 9:26
- The destruction of Jerusalem and expulsion of Jews by Hadrian AD 135
- It will occur in the last days as foretold by Jesus - *when you see standing in the holy place 'the abomination that causes desolation' spoken of through the prophet Daniel Mt 24:15*. This prophecy of Jesus referred first to the destruction of Jerusalem and also as a pattern of the end time.
- It will be the 'man of lawlessness' foretold by Paul to be revealed before the return of Jesus who will overthrow and destroy him 2Thes 2:3-12
- John defined him - the antichrist is coming - many have already come - the man who denies that Jesus is the Christ, such a man is the antichrist - he denies the Father and the Son 1Jn 2:18-22.

13:11-15 **Wonder 5 – The Beast out of the Earth** There will be **unified world ideology** – one religion binding on all *having a form of godliness but denying its power 2Tim 3:1-5*. This is personified as a beast with horns like a lamb but speaking like a dragon v11, performing miracles and mimicking Jesus v13. We see the development of this sign nationally and internationally!

This beast is the false prophet - third personage of a counterfeit of God - combining ideologies and amalgamating religious beliefs, promoting tolerance and acceptance, non-confrontational society, pleasing to the senses and degenerate morals of the ungodly v11; 16:13; 19:20; 20:10. An image will be set up and given breath - all will be required to worship it v15; Dan 3:1-6.

13:16-18 **The Mark of the Beast** All mankind will be caused to be sealed with the mark of the beast - if not they will be unable to trade v12,14,16. The saints have no need for concern for they are already sealed 7:3.

There are many explanations for this mark - 666 is the number of 'man' – one less than the prefect number 777 of the Trinity - always falling short. The number for the Greek name of Jesus is 888!

Many have sought world empire exalting themselves against or as God - the Caesars, Charlemagne, Napoleon, Kaiser, Third Reich. Many including the Reformers believe antichrist can be seen in the Roman Empire and the apostate Catholic Church - *they went out from us 1Jn*

2:19. This applies equally to other divisions of the Church who have strayed from the Word of God.

SUMMARY OF THE EVIL EMPIRE These three, the dragon and two beasts represent a final trinity of evil – a counterfeit of God's Person and of Jesus 13:1-18. There has always been conflict between good and evil. There will be a final stand of the world against God and his people. **Tribulation** Although all believers face persecution 1:9; 7:14 a final manifestation of evil will be revealed with progressive gathering of **centralized world government and ideology** symbolized by the two beasts and lead by the antichrist as mankind rejects God, culminating in great world conflict.

Israel in the mystery of God was blinded till the fullness of the Gentiles comes in - their house left desolate - then a remnant will be saved Ezk 21:25-27. The gifts of God and his call are irrevocable Mt 23:37-39; Rom 11:25-29. At the right time the faithful believers of the Church will be removed in the rapture 16:15,16; Mt 24:39-42. This final Tribulation will involve world empire and ideology against God's chosen people Israel - the time of Jacob's trouble Jer 30:4-10; Zec 12:2-5. It will be for a short time. Daniel was told that there will be seven years of Tribulation for his people of Israel - war will continue until the end of this period Dan 9:26; 12:7-13.

Great Tribulation In the middle years persecution will increase as the antichrist leads world empire against God's people as foretold by Jesus - *there will be great distress, unequaled from the beginning of the world Mt 24:21,22.* This penultimate battle is further described 16:12-16; 17:12-14; 19:19-21. In this time the seven bowls of God's wrath will be poured out on the earth. Israel will be protected, differentiated, as in Egypt Ex 8:22,23.

14:1-5 **Wonder 6 - The Second Coming of Jesus (foreseen)** The Tribulation will bring the return of Jesus to earth to defend Israel and destroy antichrist and his world empire (two beasts) Mt 24:29-32. Many Jewish people will turn to Jesus as Messiah and be saved in this period Rom 4:13. *They will look on me, the one they have pierced Zec 12:10;* Is 49:6; 62:1-5; 65:19-25 - it will no longer be *hidden from your eyes Lk 19:42.* They too will be resurrected at Jesus' return with a new everlasting covenant together with the saints of the Old Testament Jer 31:31-37; Ezk 16:60-63 - *through the Gospel the Gentiles are heirs together with Israel,* *members together of one body and sharers together in the promise in Christ Jesus Eph 3:6.*

The Lamb standing on Mount Zion with the Redeemed of Israel They are foreseen standing on Mt Zion after the defeat of the world empire and the antichrist (soon to be accomplished 19:11-16) 7:1-8; Zech 14:3-11; Rom 11:25-32.

8. SEVEN ANGELS - The Harvest of the Earth

14:6-20 **Wonder 7 - The Rapture of Believers** This event is one of the Wondrous Signs. It will be carried out by seven angels and involves the taking from earth of all who have believed in the Gospel of Jesus Christ as Savior and Lord 7:9-17. Rapture means 'caught up' 1Thes 4:17.
First Angel – the Gospel has been proclaimed throughout the earth v6.
Second Angel – Babylon, the symbol of world empire is about to fall v8.
Third Angel - all who follow the beast are identified and warned of final judgment - the last chance v9,10,11. The saints must stand firm in this period for there will be intense persecution but blessed reward v12,13.
Fourth Angel - has a sharp sickle, prepared for harvest v14. This angel will direct the angels who are sent to gather the harvest from the four winds.
Fifth Angel – gave the command to the fourth angel to go and reap the harvest of mankind. The command comes from God – **the time is now** v15. This occurs before the final wrath v19.

Earth is harvested of the saints -

The elect are gathered from the four corners of the earth v16 - just as Jesus foretold Mt 24:31. They will meet him in the air!
Now two angels prepare the nations for judgment.
Sixth Angel – has a sharp sickle ready for judgment of mankind v17.
Seventh Angel – gave the command to prepare for judgment v18 -

The Grapes of God's wrath are gathered! v19;
Is 63:3,4; Jer 25:30

The Rapture - the Day of the Lord 1Thes 5:2
Jesus will return in the air with his angels to gather believers v15,16; 1Thes 4:13-16. It will involve all born again believers of the Church age Mt 24:36-44. Believers will be caught up to meet Jesus in the air 1Thes 4:17,18.
Jesus will take them to be with him always Jn 14:1-4; 2Thes 2:1.

It will be accompanied by the sounding of the trumpet call of God - the last trump 1Cor 15:52 and the voice of the archangel 1Thes 4:13-17. It is imminent - it could happen at any moment Rom 13:12; 1Cor 15:50-54. It will occur unexpectedly 16:15; Mt 24:42-44; 1Thes 5:1-5.

It will be before the Great Tribulation, the Day of Wrath and the seven plagues of God's wrath Lk 21:34-36; 1Thes 1:10; 5:9.

Redeemed believers will not receive the end time plagues 18:4,5.

It will involve the living and dead believers 1Cor 15:22,23,51-58. They will be forever with the Lord 1Thes 4:16,17.

Believers will be transformed - made like Jesus in glory Col 3:4; 1Jn 3:2. Believers are to live in expectation of this moment Mt 25:1-13; Mk 13:32-37; Jas 5:8; 1Jn 2:18.

Unbelievers will be unaware 1Thes 5:1-5 - life on earth will continue through the Tribulation, Day of Wrath and the seven plagues Mt 24:39-41; 2Pet 3:10.

9. THE SEVEN PLAGUES - God's Wrath poured out

Again we come to the Great Day of God's Wrath 6:17; 11:18; 14:19,20. We now see the completion of God's judgment - the Third Woe 11:14.

15:1 **The third series of events** are about to proceed as the **Seven Bowls of Plagues** - they are last because with them God's wrath is complete.

15:2-5 **The Redeemed in the Presence of God** Before God's wrath is poured out another vision is given -

•   The elect of the Church era are seen gathered to God in the Harvest of the earth 14:15,16

•   The elect of Israel and the Old Covenant are secured at the Second Coming 14:1-5

•   The two Companies of 7:1,9 are now foreseen as in God's Presence. This is further confirmation and encouragement for believers of all ages 7:1-17; 14;1-20.

They sing the **'Song of Moses'** and the **'Song of the Lamb'** declaring the glory and the just, true and righteous acts of the Lord God Almighty throughout human history v3.

The Redeemed who have responded to God's call to salvation through Jesus *will not receive any of her plagues 18:4,5.*

15:5-8 **God's wrath now falls on the unrepentant** As the Seven Seals led to the **Great Day of the Lord** 6:15-17 and the Seven Trumpets led to the **time for judging the dead** 11:18 so the Seven Plagues pour out **God's wrath and punishment of sin** v8. Again God's immediate action is foreseen v5-8. The plagues come from the very Presence of God.

16:1-16 **The Seven Bowls of God's Wrath** The bowls contain Seven Plagues poured out by seven angels 15:1. These last catastrophes fulfill the **Third Woe** (from the Seventh Trumpet 11:14) and are directed against the remaining unbelievers on earth as punishment. They build on the impact of the Seven Trumpets and affect all that is important to human wellbeing. Like the plagues of Egypt Ex 7:3-5 they are intended to bring ultimate submission. However despite their ferocity people do not repent v9,11,21 -

First Plague – painful skin infections on all mankind v2

Second Plague – pollution of all the seas v3

Third Plague – pollution of all rivers v3

Fourth Plague – sun radiation and intense heat v8

Fifth Plague – darkness over the whole of the land v10

Sixth Plague – **the kings of the East, from Babylon** beyond the Euphrates gather **the kings of the whole world** at **Armageddon** in preparation for war v12-14; 17:12-14.

The Mount of Megiddo overlooks the Plain of Esdraeldon, scene of many battles – this location equates with the Valley of Jehoshaphat (the LORD judges) Joel 3:2; Zec 12:11.

The unrepentant nations are gathered by demonic, miraculous signs for the penultimate battle v14-16; 19:19-21 (ref p53) on -

The Great Day of God Almighty v14,16

Even so mankind will be caught by surprise at the return of the Lord Jesus Christ – they will still be looking for man-made security and prosperity v15; Mt 24:39; 2Pet 3:10-12.

16:17-21 **Seventh Plague – the Great City Babylon and cities of the world** Punishment is struck against the central government and ideology of the world. This will involve the catastrophic destruction of organized civilization. A voice announces from the Throne *It is done v17*; Jn 19:30.

10. THE FALL OF WORLD EMPIRE

17:1-7 **The Woman and the Beast – Insert 5** Having foreseen the fall of World Empire in overview 16:19-21 this insert now details the end of man's rebellion and independence from God. The ambition of self-centered mankind – the system of world corporate governance, is personified as a scarlet woman, adulteress, prostitute and whore guilty of gross unfaithfulness to God the Creator as well as of immorality (the two are related). Worldly splendor contrasts with profane moral corruption. The symbolic woman sits on many waters - unbelieving mankind - she sits on the beast of world empire, the antichrist v3; 13:1. **Babylon** is seen as the future material center of world commerce and of the pride of man in defiance of God - also the symbol of evil v5; 14:8; 16:19; 18:2,10,21; Gen 10:8-10. This reveals the character of world dominion and the attraction of mankind to ungodliness. Where man was created in the image of God to acknowledge and glorify him - instead mankind glorifies man!

This woman (world system) and Babylon were foreseen - compare with 'the woman in a basket' - wickedness and iniquity of the people Zec 5:5-11.

Those who are captivated by this world order are those *whose names have not been written in the Book of Life from the creation of the world v8.*

17:8-11 Progressive Empires Reviewed The seven heads of the beast represent seven mountains (symbolizing Rome, capital of the pagan world at the time of the vision). They also describe seven kings (empires) - the dragon has 7 crowns for 7 empires, the beast has 10 crowns for 10 kings 12:3; 13:1 -

• **Seven kings** Egypt was the first great empire to oppress God's people Ex 1:11. Then came Assyria 2Kin 17:5,6, Babylon 2Kin 25:21,22, Persia and Greece - these *five have fallen*

• Rome is the *one that is* in AD 90 v10

• **A seventh king *has not yet come, but when he does come, he must remain for a little while v10.*** This will be the world empire of the end time which will unite world nations and ideology - possibly out of Europe or the East. It equates with the extended 4th beast of Dan 2:33,41-43; 7:7,19-24

• **An eighth king (the beast) is the final antichrist** v11. This equates with the little horn (eleventh horn) of Dan 7:8,20-25. He is also the beast out of the sea 13:1. **He *once was, now is not, and will come up out of the Abyss and go to his destruction v8.*** He received a fatal wound that was healed 13;3;14. This is a counterfeit of Jesus 1:4-6; 5:6. He belongs to the seven (is of the same type, nature) - he comes out of the place of demons and is going to his destruction v8,11. He will be a type (resurrection) of a past evil ruler (Nimrod, Antiochus?) 13:3.

17:12 **The ten horns** Ten regional kings will arise (from the East, from Babylon, beyond the Euphrates 16:12-16) - *who have not yet received a kingdom* - they will receive authority with the beast for one hour v12. While the seven heads represent nations the antichrist will be an actual ruler, a personification of evil, a type of Nimrod of the first empire of Babylon (the cradle of civilization) Gen 10:8-10; 11:9; Mic 5:5,6.

17:13,14 **The Penultimate Battle** The antichrist (beast, eighth king) unites with the 10 kings (horns). They have one purpose - to make war against the Lamb 16:16; Zec 12:1-9. He will overcome them at his Second Coming v13,14; 19:11-21.

17:15-18 **Failure of the World System** The scarlet woman is the Great City, Babylon, the final evil empire 11:8 dominating the kings and nations of the earth in the end time v18. The antichrist beast and the 10 kings will bring her (the system) to ruin (in self-destruction) v16. We see countries in collapse today because of corrupt godless leadership. The fall of civilization will be put into the hearts of kings by God v17; Ex 9:16.

18:1-24 **The Fall of Babylon - the Great City** The pride of self-seeking mankind (the scarlet woman) will be destroyed by their own kind v15-17 – the system will fail due to the arrogance, corruption, and vindictiveness, greed and self-exaltation of the leaders. The worldly kingdoms of mankind are futile, destined to frustration and ultimate failure for they operate independent of God Gen 11:4-7. The final collapse will be complete - financial, commercial, moral, social, ecological - brought to completion by the outpouring of the Seven Plagues, an earthquake 16:18 and greed Is 13:6-13. The call to come out of the world is for today - before the plagues and destruction occur v4.

18:9-19 **The Fall of Godless Civilization** will be mourned by all who participated and put their hopes in it (her) - the kings, merchants and people. Where none could trade without the mark of the beast now none can trade!

18:20-24 **Believers will rejoice** to see justice applied as God's rule on earth arrives. Destruction will be final v21.

This series of events, the Seven Bowls (chapters 16 to 18) will be over in a short time v8,17,19. The Fifth Insert leads up to the **Battle on the Great Day of the Lord** 17:1; 19:19.

11. THE TRIUMPH of ALMIGHTY GOD and THE LAMB

19:1-8 **The Marriage of the Lamb** – **Insert 6** A description of rejoicing in heaven (the spiritual world of the heavenly realms) as the fulfilment of human history arrives. *A great multitude in heaven v1,6* the redeemed of both Covenants and the heavenly host rejoice at the victory of God over evil -
- His judgments are true and just – Hallelujah (praise God) v2
- He has avenged the blood of his servants – Hallelujah v2
- All creation now worships him – Hallelujah v4
- The Lord God omnipotent reigns – Hallelujah v6

  The time for the wedding of the Lamb has come v7

The concept of wedding describes the intimacy of relationship that the redeemed will have with the Savior for eternity Eph 5:25-27,32. Those invited have made themselves ready v7 - they put on the wedding garment of the Lamb, washed clean v8, 9. There is only one way to partake in the wedding - washed clean by the blood of the Lamb Mt 22:1-14.

19:9,10 **The testimony of Jesus is the spirit of prophecy** – the most powerful prophetic message is the plan of salvation through faith in Jesus alone. The eternal future of each person will be decided based on their response to Jesus. As he revealed God and his plan of salvation to us so we now have the privilege of revealing Jesus to others by our testimony about Jesus - by our life, words and deeds. The worship of anything apart from God is again forbidden Ex 20:3-7.

The Second Coming of Jesus

19:11-16 **The King of Kings and Lord of Lords** Jesus will appear for battle 16:16. His image, though similar to 1:12-18 is even grander for he bears his authority as Commander and Conquering King with the armies of heaven, with many crowns. The victory has already been accomplished on Calvary v13. The battle will be over in an instant for who could stand against him 1:7,17; 6:15-17. Every knee will bow and every tongue will confess that Jesus is Lord to the glory of God Phil 2:9-11. He will rule with an iron scepter v15; 12:5. The pride of mankind would see man leading the end time battle. In truth Christ will be the victor alone v15; Is 63:2-6.

19:17,18 **The Great Day of the Lord** Finally the long awaited and often foretold Day of the Lord has arrived 6:17; 11:18; 14:19; 16:14.

19:19-21 **The Great Battle** The armies of earth have gathered at **Armageddon** to do battle v19; 16:14,16; 17:12-14. It is against the LORD and his people Ps 2:1-6. The outcome is announced beforehand v17. The beast (world empire 13:1) and the false prophet (world ideology 13:11) will be cast into the eternal lake of fire and all who join the battle will be slain v21.

When Jesus returns to earth to destroy the antichrist and false prophet it will be the penultimate conflict with evil and fulfill many of the prophecies foretold Dan 7:13,14,26,27; Ezk 39:27-29; Mic 4:1-5; Zec 14:1-4,9. It will be the end time Tribulation and the Great Day of Wrath 2Thes 2:1-10; 2Pet 3:7,10; Jude 1:14,15. Jesus will appear in the clouds as conquering King of kings and very person from every nation will mourn because of him 1:7; Mt 24:30.

Many in Israel will look to Jesus as Messiah and be saved Rom 11:26,27. Those who have believed will be gathered as in the rapture 14:15,16; Mt 24:29-31.

12. THE REIGN OF JESUS

20:1-3 **Restraint of Evil** The head of the evil counterfeit 'trinity' (the devil) will be bound, completely restrained - for a period v2.

20:4-6 **MILLENIUM REIGN** v4 Old Testament writers looked forward to the messianic age of peace and justice Is 11:1-9; 62:1-12; Ezk 37:15-28. The Great Battle will be followed by the millennium rule of Christ 20:4; Zec 8:20,21. Satan will be bound for a period and later destroyed 20:2,10; 1Cor 15:24,25.

Jesus will rule mankind on earth for a period (thousand years) with an iron rod 2:27; 19:15; Ps 2:9; Is 2:1-5. It will fulfill God's promise to David and Israel that David's descendent will rule all nations from his throne on earth 1Chr 17:11-14; Ps 98:9; Is 9:6,7; 11:1-9; 32:1; 33:20-24; Jer 23:5,6; Ezk 37:24-28; Mic 4:1-4; Zec 14:1-21; Lk 1:31-33; Acts 15:13-18.

All the failed aspirations of mankind from Adam to Armageddon for a world of peace, prosperity and righteousness will be met in a moment Is 12:1-6; Amos 9:13. This period is also required as the final vindication of God's righteous judgment on sinful human nature Rom 3:19,20 - it will silence the voice of every unbeliever 3:4,19,20; Ezk 39:7,8.

20:5 **The First Resurrection** will involve those whose names are written in **the Lamb's Book of Life** from the creation of the world 13:8; 17:8; Ex 32:32; Ps 69:28; Mal 3:16; Phil 4:3. The Two Companies are already identified 7:1-17; 14:1-5,14-16. They will reign with Christ 2:26,27; 5:10.

20:7-10 **Final Destruction of Evil** Society confirms that man needs constraint – laws to bind us to do what is right and discipline us to conform – the evidence of sinful human nature. Even after experiencing the reign of Christ with all his righteous law and blessings mankind will still rebel against God!

After the millennium reign of peace the devil will be released and will deceive the remaining inhabitants on earth to turn against God. Gog and Magog (north) together with Persia (east) and Cush and Put (south and east) represent the remaining nations of the earth – these are symbolic of a previous battle Ezk 38:1-6; Zech 12:1-9. There will be no battle - they will be overcome in an instant by fire from heaven Ezk 39:1-6; Zech 14:1-4; 1Cor 15:24-28.

Satan will then be cast into the eternal lake of fire v10.

20:11-15 **The Great White Throne** The focus of human history and every eye will be on the Sovereign God and the throne of judgment committed to Jesus Mt 25:31; Jn 5:22; 2Cor 5:10. Nothing will distract from this cataclysmic event. Earth and sky flee - this will be a spiritual encounter 2Pet 3:7.

The Second Resurrection will involve unbelievers called to give account. All those not written in the Lamb's book of life will be judged by the book of deeds 20:12; Dan 12:1-3; 2Tim 4:1.

Books of Deeds Those who have denied God and his offer of salvation through Jesus will be raised and judged by their every careless word and deed v12,13; Ps 56:8; 98:8,9; 139:16; Dan 7:10; Mt 12:36,37.

Lamb's Book of Life records those who have honored God v4-6. Those whose names are not recorded will be separated from God for eternity v15; 21:27; 22:15. The eternal fire was prepared for the devil and his angels – it is the destiny of mankind only by individual choice! Mt 25:41,46; Jude 1:7.

Death and Hades will no longer be required - there will be no evil v14,15.

13. THE NEW HEAVEN and NEW EARTH – Insert 7

21:1-27 **The Throne of God and the Lamb** In contemplating the beauty of the physical universe which will pass away, one can only be filled with awe at the prospect of the existence that God has prepared for those who love him in which he makes all things new! v1; Is 34:1-4; 65:17;

Heb 1:12; 2Pet 3:7-12 - *no eye has seen, no ear has heard, no mind has conceived what God has prepared for those who love him 1Cor 2:9,10.*

Relationship with God The details of the city are lost in the glory of the intimate relationship which will exist with the Father and the Son together with the redeemed people from every nation and generation - God will dwell with them forever v3; Gen 3:8. The new Jerusalem is described as a bride indicating the people of God. As mankind was excluded from God's Presence by sin Gen 3:22 so the removal of sin provides eternal life 2:7.

There will be no tears, death, mourning, crying or pain v4 – no sea v1, no sun, moon or night v22,23. All things will be new! v5; 7:15-17.

21:6-8 **The Alpha and Omega** While the salvation of man was attained by the work of Jesus the whole plan of creation, redemption and eternal life is the work of God. He is the Alpha and Omega (first and last letters of the Greek alphabet) - the Beginning and the End of all things 1:8; Is 44:6. It is God who will supply all the needs of eternity from the spring of the water of life, without cost - by his grace. This was promised by Jesus who also uses the title 22:12,13.

21:9-27 **The Holy City** is described in physical terms in the most extravagant detail. It is a 2,500 km cube (the Sanctuary was 4.5 x 4.5 x 5m) with walls 70m thick. It is constructed in gold, pearls, precious stones v9-21.

In a Book of symbols one can appreciate that the vision is of spiritual realities in language we can understand. Wealth, splendor, limitless abundance describe the provision and the experience of the redeemed children of God for eternity. There is the exclusion of all that is evil v27.

22:1-6 **Eternal Life** The river of life was foretold Ezk 47:1-12. Eternal life is the purpose and promise of God from before the beginning of time Tit 1:2; Lev 26:12; Ezk 37:27,28. The Throne of God and of the Lamb will be in the city v3; Jer 3:17. This has always been the highest aspiration of man -

• the saints will serve God and the Lamb v3
• they will see his face v4 – they will be like him Phil 3:21
• they will reign forever and ever v5; 2:26,27; 5:10; 1Cor 6:2,3.

This is the message of the Book of Revelation - the revealing of the glorious future of those who put their faith and trust in God and his Son, Jesus Christ our Lord v6. There is no other hope of eternal life known to man.

22:7-11 **Behold, I am coming soon** We must live in expectation of the imminent return of Jesus as he encouraged us to do - we must be constantly vigilant, looking for every opportunity to extend the kingdom and tell others about him Mt 24:42-51; 25:1-13.

22:12,13 **The Deity of Jesus** is again confirmed – *I am the Alpha and the Omega, the First and the Last, the Beginning and the End* - these are the words of Jesus 1:8 – also the title of the One on the Throne 21:6; Is 44:6.

22:14-17 **Encouragement** Current readers of the Revelation are exhorted to repent while there is yet time 20:15. The offer of salvation is still open.

Jesus reemphasized that he gave the whole message of this book in vision form - that John wrote down what he actually saw and heard v16.

22:18,19 **Warning - Do Not Change, Add To or Take Away From the Prophetic Word of this Book** God has revealed all we need to know about salvation and effective living. This is a warning not to change the words of this prophetic book. A curse is pronounced on those who change, add to or take from this message. This applies to the whole of the Bible v18; Ps 119:89. Many have fallen under this curse over the generations Mt 5:17,18.

22:17-21 The response to the message of this book is unbelief or to cry – **MARANATHA - Come, Lord Jesus!**

Observation

There are a number of approaches to the Book of Revelation including -
- Preterist – the message applied primarily to the first Century
- Historicist – the message covers stages of world history to the end
- Futurist – fulfilment lies primarily at the end of the age
- Idealist - symbolic pictures of universal truths

It is not necessary to be bound by these extreme interpretations.
We must not be dogmatic about one point of view. It is important to be open to the Book and the Holy Spirit. Confirm what you conclude with other Bible verses especially in the Gospels.

There are many views on the meaning of prophecy - interesting to the enquiring mind. They must not be permitted to cause division in the Body of Christ. The primary aim is to reveal Jesus - also to encourage the believer to hold to the Word of God and to be a witness to the saving grace of God through Jesus Christ.

The message must certainly have had real meaning, comfort and encouragement for the people at the time it was written in the first century. The wonder is that it has had application for all subsequent generations in their time and also with regard to the end time. The amazing truth is that it applies to the current generation as well.

Revelation has application to the life of the church and the individual believer in the present day 1:3. God intended us to receive a message of blessing, encouragement, hope and expectation as we live for the return of Jesus. We should embrace what we read and be motivated to tell others about the necessity of salvation through faith in Jesus Christ alone!

Have you received Jesus Christ as Savior as the means of forgiveness of your sins and received the gift of eternal life? If not consider doing it now!

If you have looked for dramatic predictions of the end time you may be disappointed. If you have gained a greater insight into the glory of God and the majesty of Jesus Christ the Lord with a desire to commitment to the extension of God's kingdom then you are receiving the blessings of the Book.

End Time Timetable

Event		ref	Pattern in Revelation		ver	Pattern in Matthew 24
Seven Seals			**Opening the Scroll**		3	**Signs of the End of the Age**
General Signs	1	6.1	White Horse	Deceiver - false religion	4	False Christs - many deceived
	2	6.3	Red Horse	Takes peace from the earth	6	Wars, Rumors of war
	3	6.5	Black Horse	Poverty / Plenty / Conflict over resources	7	Nation against Nation
	4	6.8	Pale Horse	Sword / Famine / Plague, 1/3 Earth	7	Famine & Earthquake
Tribulation	5	6.9		Persecution	9	Persecution / Martyrs
Heavenly Signs	6	6.12		Earthquake, Sun, Moon, Stars	29	Sun, Moon & Stars
		6.14		Heavens & Earth Disrupted		Heavenly Bodies Shaken
		6.15		THEN Everyone Hid!	30	At that time!
Second Coming		6.17		**The Great Day of Wrath has come**	30	**The Son of Man will appear**
Insert 1	7	7.1	**Two Companies**	Israel / Gentiles - **Sealed**	31	The elect will be gathered
Seventh Seal	7	8.1	Silence in Heaven		36	When? No one knows
		8.3		Prayers of all the Saints - before the 7 Trumpets	42	Be ready!
SevenTrumpets	1	8.7		Hail & fire - 1/3 of Earth	43	I come like a thief!
	2	8.8		Sea to blood		(Compare with Rev 16:15)
	3	8.10		Rivers bitter		
Three Woes	4	8.12		Sun, Moon, Stars - 1/3 dark - (only those not sealed)		
First Woe	5	9.1		Locusts - Torment		
Second Woe	6	9.13		Angels, Troop - 1/3 of Mankind		
		9.20		**Rest of Mankind still did not repent**		
Insert 2		10.1	**Witness of the Saints**			
		10.3		Seven Thunders - The Mystery of God will be accomplished Eph 1:9,10		
		10.8		An open Scroll - sweet & sour - we must proclaim the Gospel		
Insert 3		11.1	**Two Witnesses**	Last Testimony to the fallen world		
Third Woe	7	11.15	**Heaven is opened - God's kingdom replaces the kingdom of the world**			
		11.18	**The time has come for judging the dead & rewarding your saints**			
Insert 4		12.1	**An Overview - Israel & the Chruch - victorious**			
Seven Wonders	1	12.1	A Woman - Israel			
	2	12.3	A Dragon - Satan			
	3	12.5	A Child who will rule - with an iron septre - Jesus			

Group	#	Ref	Description	LEGEND
		12.6	The Woman fled - The Dragon cast down	**LEGEND**
		12.13	The Woman pursued	
		12.17	The rest of her offspring were pursued (the Church)	
	4	13.1	**A beast out of the sea - World Empire**	**Story Line** - skeleton of History
		13.7	Given power to conquer the Saints	- the Seals, Trumpets,
		13.8	All people will worship World Empire - except the Saints	Wonders, Angels & Plagues.
		13.10	Persecution - endurance	
	5	13.11	**A beast out of the earth - World Ideology**	**Inserts - 7**
	6	14.1	**The Lamb on Mt Zion - Israel Elect** (identified)	Describe events, people,
Seven Angels	7,1	14.6	Gospel Proclaimed - the last chance	A period in the story
	2	14.8	Judgement on the World Order is announced	Not in the storyline - appear
	3	14.9	Judgement on all who follow the World Ideology	when needed to explain
	4,5	14.14	Harvest of Mankind - **Rapture**	
	6,7	14.17	Grapes of Wrath gathered	**Seals - 7**
		15.2	**Redeemed - victorious over the Beast**	The plan for the End Time could
Seven Plagues	1	16.1	**Pour out God's Wrath**	not be carried out till the Lamb
	2	16.2	Torment	was slain & returned to heaven
	3	16.3	Sea	
	4	16.4	**Rivers - You are just in judgments**	**Trumpets - 7**
	5	16.8	Sun - They refused to repent	Herald the coming judgement
	6	16.10	Darkness - They refused to repent	
	7	16.12	Rivers dried - Evil Spirits - Kings of the Whole World gather	**Wondrous Signs - 7**
		16.14	**Battle of the Great Day of God Almighty** - Armagedon	Significant persons & events in
Insert 5		17.1	**The Triumph of God Almighty**	history
		17,18	A woman on the Beast - fall of Babylon (world order)	
		19.1	**King of Kings & Lord of Lords! - the Second Coming**	**Angels - 7** Rev 19:10; 22:9
Insert 6		19.6	**Marriage of the Lamb**	Harvest of the elect
		20.4	**The First Resurrection - Lamb's Book of Life**	**Plagues (Bowls) - 7**
		20.7	Satan bound	The outpouring of God's wrath
		20.4	**The Reign of Christ - a thousand years**	
		20.7	Satan's release & doom (cf. 19:20)	
		20.11	**The Second Resurrection - judged by their deeds**	
Insert 7		21.1	New Jerusalem	
		22.1	**Throne of God & the Lamb will be with his servants!**	**Maranatha - Come, Lord Jesus!**

Revelation Overview Ch 7 to 22

1 7 SEALS - Ch 6

S1	Religions
S2	Wars
S3	Poverty
S4	Famine
S5	Persecution
S6	Heavenly Signs
S7	Seal 7

Great Day of God's Wrath 6:17

2 INSERT 1 - Ch 7

2 Companies - Redeemed Old & New Covenant - sealed 7:2,3

3 7 TRUMPETS - Ch 8

T1	land
T2	sea
T3	rivers
T4	heavens
T5	evil
T6	Rest of mankind did not repent 9:20
T7	Trumpet 7 - 11:15

Time for Judgment 11:18

4 INSERT 2

Witness of the Saints 10:1-11

5 INSERT 3

2 Heavenly Witnesses 11:1-14

6 INSERT 4 - Ch 12,13 / 7 WONDERS - Ch 12,13

W1	Woman
W2	Dragon
W3	Child / Satan Cast Out
W4	Beast 1 - World Empire 13:1
W5	War on the Saints 13:7 / Beast 2 - Ideology 13:11
W6	The Lamb & Redeemed 14:1-5
W7	Harvest of the earth

7 7 Angels - Ch 14:6-20

A1	Gospel preached v6,7
A2	Fall of empire declared v8
A3	Final warning v9-13
A4	Harvest of the elect v14
A5	Rapture v15,16
A6	Sickle
A7	God's Wrath 14:17-20

8 7 PLAGUES - Ch 15,16

God's wrath is complete 15:1

P1	torment
P2	seas
P3	rivers
P4	sun
P5	darkness
P6	prepare for war
P7	Great Battle 16:14

Redeemed 15.2

9 INSERT 5 - Ch 17

- Triumph of God
- Scarlet Woman
- Beast 13:1,11
- Fall of Babylon

Redeemed 19.1

10 INSERT 6 - Ch 19

- Second Coming
- King of Kings
- Great Battle 19:19
- Satan bound 20:1
- 1st Resurrection
- 1000 years reign 20:1-6
- Satan released - Final conflict 20:7-9

11 INSERT 7 - Ch 21,22

- 2nd Resurrection - Judgment 20:12
- New Jerusalem - God dwells with His people!

Outline of the Epistles

Epistles of Paul

Epistle	date	from	theme
First Mission Journey			
Galatians	AD 49	Antioch	Freedom from the Law through faith in Christ Jesus.
Second Mission Journey			
1 Thessalonians	AD 51	Corinth	Holiness of living. Christ's return.
2 Thessalonians	AD 51	Corinth	The Day of the Lord's return.
Third Mission Journey			
1 Corinthians	AD 55	Ephesus	Instruction in daily living & spiritual gifts
2 Corinthians	AD 56	Macedonia	Guidelines in discipleship
Romans	AD 57	Corinth	God's gift of righteousness by faith in Christ alone
Prison Epistles			
Ephesians	AD 60	Rome	New life in Christ. Spiritual warfare
Philippians	AD 60	Rome	The joy of living for Christ.
Colossians	AD 60	Rome	The supremacy of Christ & the Gospel
Philemon	AD 60	Rome	Forgiveness.
Further Journeys & Prison			
1 Timothy	AD 63	Macedonia	Leadership Manual
Titus	AD 63	Macedonia	Conduct for Christian Living
2 Timothy	AD 66	Rome	Endurance in pastoral ministry

General Epistles

Epistle	date	from	theme
Hebrews	AD 65	unknown	The Gospel of Jesus Christ is superior to the Old Covenant in all respects
James	AD 48	Jerusalem	Genuine faith produces action
1 Peter	AD 55	Jerusalem	The glory of the believer's inheritance
2 Peter	AD 65	Rome	Warning against false teaching.
1 John	AD 90	Patmos	Deity of Jesus & assurance of salvation
2 John	AD 90	Patmos	Continue in love as we follow Jesus.
3 John	AD 90	Patmos	Be faithful in leadership.
Jude	unknown	Jerusalem	Beware of false teachers.
Revelation	AD 90	Patmos	Sovereignty of God & return of Jesus

	BOOKS OF THE BIBLE		
	[39 + 27 = 66]		
	BOOKS OF THE OLD TESTAMENT		
	[39]		
	HISTORY (17)	POETRY (5)	PROPHECY (17)
LAW (5)	Genisis	Job	Isaiah	MAJOR (5)
Pentateuch	Exodus	Psalms	Jeremiah	
Books of Moses	Leviticus	Proverbs	Lamentations	
	Numbers	Ecclesiastes	Ezekiel	
	Deuteronomy	Solomon	Daniel	
HISTORY (12)	Joshua		Hosea	MINOR (12)
of Israel	Judges		Joel	
	Ruth		Amos	
	1 Samuel		Obadiah	
	2 Samuel		Jonah	
	1 Kings		Micah	
	2 Kings		Nahum	
	1 Chronicles		Habakkuk	
	2 Chronicles		Zephaniah	
	Ezra	Post Exile	Haggai	
	Nemiah		Zechariah	
	Esther		Malachi	

	BOOKS OF THE NEW TESTAMENT		
	[27]		
	HISTORY (5)	LETTERS OF PAUL (13)	GENERAL LETTERS (9)
GOSPELS (4)	Matthew	Romans	Hebrews	Unknown
	Mark	1 Corinthians	James	Other
	Luke	2 Corinthians	1 Peter	Apostles (7)
	John	Glatians	2 Peter	
Early Church (1)	Acts	Ephesians	1 John	
Luke		Philippians	2 John	
		Colossians	3 John	
		1 Thessalonians	Jude	
		2 Thessalonians	Revelation	John
		1 Timothy		
		2 Timothy		
		Titus		
		Philemon		

"The Layman's Commentary Series contains the following -

Volume 1 – Book of the Law
Volume 2 – Books of History
Volume 3 – Books of Wisdom
Volume 4 – Books of the Prophets
Volume 5 – Books of the Gospels
Volume 6 – Acts of the Apostles
Volume 7 – Epistles of Paul
Volume 8 – General Epistles"